D1524605

KITCHEN CANDLECRAFTING

Ruth Monroe

KITCHEN CANDLECRAFTING

South Brunswick and New York: A. S. Barnes and Company
London: Thomas Yoseloff Ltd

Library of Congress Catalogue Card Number: 72-85193

A.S. Barnes and Company, Inc.
Cranbury, New Jersey 08512

Thomas Yoseloff Ltd
108 New Bond Street
London W1Y OQX, England

First Printing December, 1969
Second Printing November, 1970
Third Printing June, 1971

ISBN: 0-498-06853-6

Printed in the United States of America

CONTENTS

INTRODUCTION

CANDLES have come a long way from the utilitarian lengths of tallow and string used by our grandparents. Most homes have a few household candles tucked away in a drawer for emergency use when the electricity fails, but the majority of candles around today are displayed proudly.

Whether you are a novice hobbyist or an old pro, candlecrafting can give your creative urge wide scope. Artistic talent, although definitely an asset, is not necessary for making beautiful candles.

The selling of handcrafted candles is an excellent way to raise money for churches, clubs, or other organizations. Many retirees, housewives, and even partially handicapped persons supplement their income with candles made in their kitchens. Some of these people have built up excellent home-candle businesses with no more talent, time, or ingenuity than you have.

Milk-carton candles have added their glow to Christmas for many years, but it took two sheet-metal workers from Seattle to put candlecrafting on a year-round basis. Don and Ray Olson made some metal molds for their mother in response to her request for something better than milk cartons. These molds changed their lives and opened up a whole new world for the hobbyist. Friends and neighbors clamored for their own molds; the clamor spread, and the end result was the Pourette Manufacturing Company. This was the first concern to offer professional, workable molds to the craftsman, and everyone who enjoys working with wax is indebted to the Olson brothers.

With the introduction of the metal mold, the stubborn souls who had struggled with milk cartons for years became avid candlecrafters. They experimented and perfected decorating techniques. Because of the demand for their unusual candles, many found their hobby could be quite profitable.

As this hobby grew, so did the availability of quality materials needed to make the candle burn properly as well as please the eye. Makeshift methods such as using string for a wick or crayons for coloring are no longer necessary. Today special candle dyes are obtainable in a wide assortment of colors; professional candle wicking has replaced the string; and stearic acid, crystals, excellent candle waxes, and other supplies are easy to obtain.

The technical aspects of candlemaking will be left to the chemists. In this book you will find no formulas for waxes, making your own wick, or manufacturing candle dyes. Instead, you will be given clear and understandable instructions for using the excellent materials available, with enough ideas on the mechanics and artistry of decorating to get you started and stir your imagination.

So, if you have ever visited a candle shop, peeked at the price tags, sighed and gone home empty-handed, make your own candles at home for fun, for gifts, or for extra cash.

KITCHEN CANDLECRAFTING

I

MOLDS AND MATERIALS

CANDLE molds are usually thought of as being of fairly recent origin, but tin and pewter molds were in general use around the middle of the 17th century. These were utility molds and their primary purpose was to ease the never-ending task of providing light. They enabled candles to be mass produced on a limited scale, and for housewives who could afford to buy their candles, itinerant chandlers would come to homes and stay long enough to mold the winter's supply.

The metal molds of today are a different story. They are lightweight and easy to handle. These molds are engineered so there is no difficulty in removing the candle and they come in all sizes and shapes. New molds are constantly appearing on the market and there is a mold to suit almost any fancy—short ones, tall ones, fat ones and skinny ones, tapered and straight, crimped and plain. (Illustration No. 1.)

If cartons have been the molds for your previous efforts with wax, a delightful surprise is waiting for you when you remove your first candle from a metal mold. Even with the flaws common to the inexperienced candlemaker, this candle will be far superior to others you may have produced. Using professional metal molds, the wax is poured at a much higher temperature than is possible in a milk carton and the result is a candle with a glass-like sheen. Working at your kitchen stove, you can turn out candles that even the most expensive machines can't match.

Mass production is one of the marvels of our age, and the right equipment can make hundreds of good, functional candles each day. Oddly enough, this works to the advantage of the craftsman. As the ever-rising flood of machine-produced articles reaches the market place, more and more discriminating people turn to

Illustration No. 1. Some of the many varieties of candle molds. (Photo by Darst-Ireland)

objects that have been lovingly and painstakingly created by skilled hands. The ability of machines to spew out a magnitude of goodies is unquestioned, but the craftsman is master of the machine when quality is the prime objective. So don't feel that just because mass production can do it cheaper, it can do it better.

The one area where mass production is welcomed in candlecrafting is in the manufacturing of metal molds. Quantity production usually means lower prices and the mold is one of the basic tools of the candlemaker.

In addition to making lovely candles, the metal mold has the added plus of being exceptionally durable. With a minimum of care, it willl last a lifetime. Dry it after each use to eliminate the possibility of rust and cover it with a plastic bag when storing to keep out dust and dirt. Never, never strike your mold with a sharp object, as even a small dent will cause difficulty in removing the candle. Molds are not expensive, so let your friends buy their own instead of borrowing yours. It is very seldom that a loaned mold will return to its owner in the same condition it left home. Any scratches made by trying to remove wax from the inside of the mold with a sharp or pointed object will be reproduced on the candle. If the simple rules above are followed, your mold will function perfectly for many years.

As wonderful as the metal molds are, they do have limitations. Intricate curves or designs reproduced in metal would increase the cost of the molds considerably, so inexpensive plastic and plaster take over where the metal molds leave off. There is almost no design that can't be reproduced by these two molds.

The first plastic molds left much to be desired, as the wax couldn't be poured too hot for fear of melting the mold. Many a disgruntled candlecrafter has had the mold split open after filling, spilling wax over a wide area. Even with their imperfections, the plastic molds do fill a definite need in candle creating, and there is evidence that some really good plastic molds will soon be on the market.

The plaster, or ceramic mold is a joy, as much topflight artistic talent has gone into the designing of these molds. Small molds, from which wax castings are used for decorating candles, are excellent and inexpensive. The large plaster molds are usually quit costly and, unless the hobby becomes a business, are generally avoided by the home candlecrafter. An all-wax candle, including decorations, is preferred by many and there is a plaster mold to fill any decorating need.

There are other molds that become molds only when used as such. Muffin tins, salad molds, drinking glasses, pilsner glasses, tin cans, plastic flower pots and bottles of plastic or glass are just a few of the items cluttering up the average household which may be converted to candle molds.

For the individualist who wants something different, it is possible to make a mold of your own design or any other object that is not copyrighted. This is done with a special liquid rubber that has been developed to withstand the high heat of molten wax.

Wax

The first step in making a candle is having a mold, but what goes into that mold is of equal importance. The proper wax is essential if your candle is to perform efficiently as well as be decorative. When nothing better than grocery store paraffin was available, it had to do, but commercial candle waxes are now easy to obtain and what a difference in results. These waxes have a wide melting-point range and can fill almost any candlemaking need.

Different melting-point waxes are needed for various types of candles. For a candle to be poured in a metal mold, a melting point of 143 to 165 degrees is desirable. Container candles (candles poured and burned in glass) work better when a lower melting point wax is used—125 to 135 degrees. The use of wax with a melting point between 160 and 170 degrees results in a hurricane candle less susceptible to heat-softened sides.

The above list of melting-point ranges is approximate, as melting points of waxes will vary with the manufacturer. The range differential is slight however, and seldom varies more than 5 degrees. Experimenting with different waxes to find the one that works best for you is strongly recommended.

Candle wax may be ordered from any of the candle supply houses, but wax is heavy and so are freight charges. It is more economical to buy wax locally if at all possible. Some of the houses, knowing that freight costs often exceed the cost of the wax, will furnish a list of nearby places where you may get your wax. Most of the oil companies manufacture candle waxes as a petroleum by-product. Check with you local petroleum products distributor to find a nearby source. In response to the demands for candlemaking supplies, hobby shops are enlarging their stocks to include all the materials needed for this craft and wax can often be obtained from them.

Beeswax

Beeswax is not used extensively by the candle hobbyist because of its expense and the problem of getting it out of the mold. It is a soft and rather sticky wax, and this tackiness prohibits easy mold release. However, beeswax is one of the highest quality waxes obtainable and produces candles of exceptional beauty and function. Most church candles contain at least 50 percent beeswax and many are hand-rolled candles made from pure beeswax. For the fortunate few who have beeswax easily available, it may be added to regular candle wax in proportions up to 50 percent, or regular candle wax may be poured into the mold. After 10 or 15 minutes, pour the still-liquid wax from the mold and fill the cavity with beeswax. The thin shell of regular wax will come out of the mold easily and the beeswax portion of the candle will burn like a dream.

Wick

Back in the dark ages of the carton candle, a string of any thickness was placed in the mold and that was your wick. It smoked, or sometimes didn't burn at all. If it did burn, it had an unpleasant habit of flickering and dying after a short time. The now readily available professional candle wicking has had a great deal to do with the improvement of the hobbyist's candles. The proper size and type of wick is of great importance to the proper burning of your candle. Wick too small for the diameter of the candle may cause the flame to be drowned in melted wax and will cause excessive dripping. A wick too large will smoke. No attempt will be made here to go into details concerning the types and sizes of wicks. All mold suppliers list the correct sizes of wick to be used with each of their molds, and countless tests have been run to assure the best performance with a certain mold.

Stearic Acid

Stearic acid, or stearine as it is sometimes called, was almost as much of a boon to the candle industry as the discovery of paraffin. Added to wax, it makes a harder, more opaque, and better burning candle. The amount to be added to wax is somewhat a matter of personal preference. The more stearic acid added, the greater the opaqueness of the finished candle. A proportion of ⅔ untinted wax and ⅓ stearic acid will result in a snow-white appearance. If a more translucent candle is wanted, the amount of stearic acid is reduced. Two or three tablespoons of stearic acid added to wax will improve the qualities of the wax considerably, but will allow a more translucent effect.

Stearic acid is harmless and has none of the burning qualities associated with many acids. It may be handled with complete safety and will not damage clothing or skin in any way.

Crystals

Crystals are another additive, which, while not essential, increase the beauty of the finished candle. A teaspoonful added to a couple of pounds of wax will produce a hard, glistening surface, as well as improved burning qualities. These are sold under various trade names, but are generally known simply as "crystals."

Dye

Modern candle dyes are a far cry from the crayons formerly used by the hobbyist to color candles. All the basic colors are available and these can be mixed to achieve any shade or tint. If you aren't in the mood to mix colors, the supply houses will do it for you. They offer dye buds in such a range of shades that the only thing left for you to do is shave off the necessary amount and put it in your wax. Dyes come in liquid, powder, and solid forms. The liquids and powders are usually sold in the basic colors and the solid dye, or dye bud, is prepared from the other dyes and pre-mixed for color selection.

When using powdered dye, it should be dissolved in a small amount of hot wax and allowed to harden. When several dye colors are prepared in this manner, place each color in a small container—a clean tomato sauce can is fine for this purpose—and label each can with a felt marker or a piece of tape. Small pieces can be cut from the hardened dye when needed.

Liquid dye is usually put in the wax with a dropper. This dye is particularly good when you want to exactly duplicate a color in a previously made candle. If a record is kept of the number of drops of color added to a certain amount of wax, the same color can be repeated in any number of candles.

Color buds are the easiest and most widely used of all dyes. Small pieces are shaved off the bud and dropped into hot wax until the desired color intensity is achieved.

Because of the keen competition and the need to cut costs wherever possible to meet this competition, many commercial candle companies color only the outside of the candle. This is done by dipping candles in different colors of wax so they acquire tinted shells. This is not recommended except for special effects. For example, it is annoying to light a big, fat, red Christmas candle and find when the top coat of wax burns off that you have a white candle with a minute amount of red wax on the outside.

Scent

Nothing is more delightful and unexpected than to light a lovely candle and suddenly realize that it smells good too. So for a candle that "smells as good as it looks," add your favorite scent. That bottle of perfume on your dresser can't be used for this because it has an alcohol base. An oil base is necessary for lasting fragrance in a candle. The only restriction on the aroma emitted by your burning candle is your preference. Flower scents, fruit, spice, French perfumes, pine, cedar, balsam, leather, and bayberry are just a fraction of the wide and varied range of perfumes that can make a candle an aromatic delight. There are also insect repelling scents such as citronella for outdoor use.

A charming gift for a hospitalized friend is a scented candle, preferably something with a clean, fresh smell. Scented candles can also clear a room of unpleasant odors left over from cooking or smoking.

2

MAKING THE CANDLE

TWO items that were not mentioned previously and that are important in your candlemaking operation are plenty of newspapers and old clothes.

The old clothes, or a smock or large apron, eliminate the problem of what to do about spilled wax on good wearing apparel. If you do pour wax in your best dress and the inevitable wax splatters occur, don't despair. If the garment can only be dry cleaned, scrape off as much wax as possible and send it to the cleaner, telling him what caused the stain. If the material is washable and colorfast, remove all the wax you can and hold the stained spot under the hot water tap, with water at hottest possible temperature. Placing the garment between paper towels and pressing with a hot iron will also remove most of the wax.

Spreading newspapers over your working area before you begin your candlemaking will save much time that would otherwise be spent scraping up spilled and dropped wax. When you are finished, the newspapers can be gathered up and dropped in the trash, with only minor cleanup being necessary. If waxed paper is placed over newspaper at points where the greatest spillage of wax is likely to occur, the hardened wax can be removed from the paper and used again. Wax spilled on newspaper absorbs the ink and becomes unsuitable for reuse.

Most candle wax is sold in slabs weighing approximately ten pounds each. These slabs must be broken into pieces that are small enough to fit into your melting pot. As wax is quite brittle, it can be quickly and easily broken into fragments by pounding with a hammer. Unused pieces can be wrapped in plastic (bags that are placed over your cleaned clothes by dry cleaners are excellent for this) to keep them clean.

Wax is a flammable substance and should never be heated directly over an open flame. Melting pot may be set in a pan of water or on one of the asbestos or metal pads that fit over the burner and equalize the heat. There are two reasons for this precaution; one is the possibility of wax igniting and the other is to melt the wax without scorching it. If wax is heated too fast or at too high a temperature, it turns a dirty brown color. Wax should not be left unattended for long periods of time and any melted wax should be wiped from the outside of the melting container to avoid the possibility of its dripping into the stove.

A wax fire is not a common occurrence and most people will spend a lifetime without experiencing one. The reason it is mentioned here is because there is a possibility one might happen. If it is handled correctly, nothing more serious than a dirty stove will result. In the event a fire should occur, water should never be used to extinguish it; instead smother the fire with a pot lid or sprinkle with baking soda. A good idea is to fill a spray gun—the kind used for spraying bugs—with soda and always have it near your melting wax.

Any container that is leak-proof and will withstand heat may be used for a melting pot. Many people use a coffee can with one side bent to form a spout. However, the easy-to-grip handle and convenient pouring spout make a coffee pot the favorite utensil of most candlecrafters. An inexpensive pot from the dime store will perform as satisfactorily as a more costly one.

Size of melting pot is a matter of personal preference, but a large 16-cup coffee pot will hold enough wax to make two or three candles, depending on their sizes. For just one candle, a small pot is entirely adequate, but for casting several candles at one pouring, a large container makes quantity production a lot easier and quicker.

After wax has been broken into pieces, place pieces in your melting container. Put container in a pan of water or on a pad on your stove and allow wax to melt. As wax melts, you will have to add more wax pieces to bring wax to the desired level. Allow at least 2″ between the top of melted wax and top of container to facilitate easy pouring. Wax is hard to control when pouring and will run over the top of container as well as out of the pouring spout if pot is filled to the top. Besides causing air bubbles in your candle, this can make a real mess.

There is a slight difference in using the medium temperature (143 to 150 degree) wax and the higher temperature (160 to 165 degree) wax, and which one you use more or less depends on which is the easiest to come by and which gives you the type of candles you want. For years I used almost nothing but the 143-150 degree wax and was very happy with it until I got hold of a bad batch of wax (it happens occasionally). Time was short and there were orders to fill and all I could obtain was some 160-165 degree wax. After trying different combinations of wax, stearic, and crystals, I decided I liked it even better than the other wax and now use it for most candles.

If you decide to begin with the 143-150 degree wax, by all means use stearic acid in proportions to obtain the opaqueness you want. Add the stearic acid to wax after wax in your container has melted.

Crystals melt at a higher temperature than waxes and it is best to melt them separately. They can be put in a small container, such as a can, and covered with very hot wax or can be mixed with a little wax and placed on the stove until they melt. Wax and melted crystals are then poured into the melting pot.

I have found that with the higher melting point wax, the addition of crystals alone produces better results than when stearic is also added. This is what works best for me with the wax I use, but definitely doesn't mean that it will work best for you. Although you use a wax with the same melting point, it might be from a different source and it will not react exactly the same as the wax I use. So, at the risk of repeating myself again and again, please don't be afraid to experiment with different combinations of basic ingredients to find what pleases you. There are very few hard and fast rules in candlecrafting and even the weather can have an effect on your candlemaking.

When wax is melted and at the right temperature for pouring, dye is added. Candle dyes are highly concentrated and should be added sparingly until the desired color is obtained. By peering into a pot of melted wax, it is impossible to judge its color, but a few drops of hot colored wax on a white saucer or in a bowl of cold water will give an approximate idea of the color of the finished candle. The finished candle will usually be a slightly deeper color because of its density, but the difference will be minor. If, after testing your color in the above manner, you want it darker, gradually add more dye, testing each time. If you goof and put in too much dye, pour off some of the colored wax and add clear wax to reduce the intensity of color.

Once you put the dye in your wax, stay by the stove. Many dyes will change color if exposed to heat for long periods, so get your wax off the stove as soon as dye has melted and you have the color you want. Stir wax before pouring to be certain dye and wax are thoroughly mixed.

The addition of scent can be accomplished by several methods. The most common is to put the scent in your melting pot just prior to pouring into the mold. Another way is to add it to the wax that is used to refill candle, or wick may be dipped in scent before being placed in mold.

A pleasant fragrance and not an overpowering odor is usually desired, so use no more than a teaspoon of scent until your own preference has been established.

The foregoing instructions are general and apply to almost all candles. Now we leave the generalities and concern ourselves with pouring into specific types of molds.

Pouring in Metal Molds

A clean mold is a must for perfect candles. Dust or lint will cause blemishes on the candle surface. Candle supply houses have a special solvent for cleaning dirty molds, or regular dry cleaning fluid may be used. Mold is easily cleaned by plugging the hole in bottom and pouring in a small amount of cleaner. Place your hand over the opening of mold and swirl the cleaner around the inside. Don't throw this cleaner away after you've slicked up your mold; pour it back in the bottle and use it again. For stubborn areas of hardened wax, dip a soft cloth in cleaner and scrub gently.

While wax is heating, assemble your mold for pouring so it will be ready when wax reaches correct temperature. Using the correct size wick for the mold, dip tip of wick into hot wax. Wait a few seconds and then draw the tip of wick between thumb and forefinger to straighten it. When wax hardens, wick will be rigid and easier to thread through the wick hole in bottom of mold.

Turn mold upside down and push wick through hole. Pull

wick to top of mold and tie it to a pencil or the metal rod that is included with most molds. Place this rod across top of mold, pull wick taut from the bottom and insert screw in mold. Cut wick so it extends about 2" beyond the wick hole and wind this remaining wick around the screw. With a table knife or small screwdriver, tighten screw and place a small piece of modeling clay or electrician's tape over the screw and wick, pressing it down on all sides to prevent wax leakage. An extra second or so spent on this step to be sure there is no small hole left for wax to leak out of or water to seep into will be well worth the effort.

The making of a candle with a smooth, professional surface requires a warm mold when pouring wax. There are several methods of warming molds. One is to place mold in oven which has been heated to 150 or 175 degrees—no higher—and allow mold to remain until it is warm. Too much heat may soften or melt the solder used to hold mold together. Mold may also be warmed by running hot water over the outside, being careful that no water gets into the interior of mold. The best, easiest, and quickest way to warm a mold is with a hair dryer. Insert the blower hose in mold, turn the dryer on hot and mold is warmed in seconds. With this method, there is no danger of forgetting there is a mold in the oven and no possibility of water splashing into mold.

Temperature of wax at time of pouring plays an important part in creating a perfect candle. For metal molds the recommended temperature is between 180 and 200 degrees. An inexpensive candy or deep fat thermometer from the dime store inserted in hot wax will tell at a glance when correct temperature has been reached and eliminates guesswork.

Now wax is at the correct temperature, dye and scent have been added, mold is warm, and everything is ready for the first pouring. Grasp the mold with a hot pad or towel to protect your hands from burns, tilt mold slightly, and pour wax slowly down the inside of mold. If mold is tilted while wax is being poured, it reduces the possibility of wax splashing into mold and creating air bubbles. Air bubbles are the bugaboo of the candlemaker as they cause unsightly pit marks in an otherwise perfect candle. Pour wax almost to top of mold, gradually bringing mold back to an upright position as it fills. After pouring, allow mold to sit for a minute or two to permit any air bubbles to rise to the surface. Gently tapping the mold with a rubber scraper or some other object that will not dent mold will help dislodge air bubbles also.

As wax congeals in the mold it will shrink and must be refilled. Save at least ½ cup of wax of original color for this refilling.

Sometimes even with careful preparation, wax will leak from the hole in mold bottom. This leakage can be quickly stopped by having a pan containing an inch or so of cold water nearby. Place the leaking mold in the water and wax will harden enough to prevent further leakage.

A word of caution—when pouring wax, don't let it get near your sink drain. Drain pipes and congealed wax are not compatible and usually a plumber is needed to get everything working again.

The Water Bath

The water bath is the next step and it is vital to the good looks of your candle. It gives a finish not obtainable any other way. Some people say they get the same results by skipping the water bath, but it doesn't work for most of us. Try it both ways before you decide to bypass this step.

Fill a container wider and taller than the mold with lukewarm water to within about 1″ of the top of mold. Hold top of mold with a hot pad and gently lower it into water. The larger molds have a tendency to float and it may be necessary to use a weight of some sort to hold them in place. Be very careful not to allow water to get into mold.

A large plastic wastebasket makes an excellent water bath container as it is lightweight, waterproof, and can be filled to accommodate short or tall molds. It also has the added advantage of being just translucent enough so that when a mold is placed against it on the outside, it is possible to accurately judge how far to fill the container.

If there was a miscalculation and not enough water was put in the container before immersing mold, do not add more water after the mold is in. The result will be bubbly lines on the candle where water was added.

Leave candle in water until a thick film forms across the top and an indentation appears around the wick. Remove candle from water and punch two or three deep holes in wax close to wick. Be sure wick is in the center of candle; otherwise when it is burned the flame will consume more wax on one side of candle than on the other and cause wax to drip on this side. If you have any shiskebab skewers around the house, they are perfect for punching your holes. If not, a pencil or thin stick will do.

Pour hot wax saved from the first pouring into the holes until well or depression is almost filled. Do not fill all the way to top of candle as wax may run down between sides of mold and candle, making candle hard to release and ruining its finish. It will be necessary to refill candle two or three times to be sure all air pockets are eliminated. Cooling wax shrinks and forms a vacuum. If candle is not refilled, there will be holes inside the candle or a cave-in or depression on side of candle.

Let candle stand until mold is completely cool to the touch before trying to remove it. This will take several hours, but be patient. If it is impossible to wait that long, place candle in refrigerator for an hour or so, but don't let it get too cold or wax is likely to crack. This is an emergency measure only, as it is better to let wax cool gradually.

When wax is cold, turn mold upside down, remove clay or tape, unwind the screw and candle should slide out. If it doesn't, pound the top of mold gently on a folded towel to avoid damaging the mold. If candle still won't come out, place mold in refrigerator for 30 minutes or an hour and try again. The last resort is holding the mold under the hot water tap. The hot water will cause the sides of candle to melt enough so it can be pulled out of the mold. The candle is ruined of course, but it is out of the mold and can be remelted and poured again.

Normally, there is no problem in removing a candle from the mold, but if you have trouble with sticking candles, try one of the silicone mold-release sprays available at candle supply houses. However if a good grade of wax is used and care is taken when it is poured, the mold should seldom need to be treated. If you consistently have trouble with candles releasing, try another wax and see if that may be the solution.

That candle you have just removed from the mold and are now admiring may look perfect, but there are a few finishing touches needed to make the job complete. The seam line on the mold has produced a corresponding seam line in the wax and this has to be trimmed off. This can be done in a flash by running a sharp knife down the seam line to remove the excess wax.

Sometimes the base of candle must be leveled so candle will stand straight. A knife may also be used for this task, but for a more professional looking result, rotate the candle on a flat heated surface. One of the most efficient methods of leveling the bottom of a candle is to use two pie or cake pans, one smaller than the other, and turn the small one upside down in the larger one. Cover the bottom of the large pan with water and heat water until it boils. When the candle bottom is rotated on the upside-down tin, the melting wax will run off the pan and into the water. After water is cold, hardened wax may be lifted out of the water.

Rubbing the bottom of a candle over a cheese grater will level it in a hurry. Candle can then be rotated on a heated pan a couple of times to smooth out the grater ridges.

Small circles of felt placed on the bottom of candles will cover any unsightliness and also protect furniture.

Trim wick to a length of ¼″ to ½″ and candle is finished and ready for decorating or burning as is.

Hurricane Molds

A hurricane candle is not really a candle, but a thin shell of wax inside which a votive candle is burned. The use of a hurricane candle is one of the few ways in which you can have your candle and burn it too. Hurricane molds are usually made of metal like the regular candle molds; the only difference being that they are shorter and fatter and there is no hole in the bottom for a wick.

A hurricane candle is made the same as a regular candle up to a point. The procedure is identical, except that no wick is used, until after it has been placed in the water bath. As soon as a film about ⅛″ thick forms on the top of the candle, remove mold from the water bath. Insert a knife in this congealed wax about ¼″ from the mold edge and cut out and remove the center wax. Pour the liquid wax inside the mold back into the melting pot.

It's easy to get busy and forget about your candle reclining in its water bath, and by the time you remember it, the shell may be thicker than you want. To correct this situation, refill the shell with very hot wax while candle is still in mold. Allow wax to stand in shell for a few seconds. This hot wax will melt some of the wax on inside of shell, making shell thinner. A thin shell is desirable so that the light of the votive candle may be seen. The hot wax pouring also smooths the inside of the shell.

If desired, a different color wax may be used for this second pouring and will result in a shade on the inside different from the balance of the shell.

Turn mold upside down to allow any excess wax to drain. This also prevents the sides from sagging before the wax has hardened. When wax is firm but not hard, cut a round hole in the bottom of candle with a cookie cutter.

Except in rare instances, the top of the shell will be ragged and badly, in need of smoothing. After candle is removed from mold, a knife may be used for trimming or the top of the shell placed on a hot pan and excess wax melted off.

The circle cut in the bottom of the candle with the cookie cutter may be easily pushed out when wax has hardened. The reason for this hole is to allow the placing of the shell over a lighted votive candle rather than risk burned fingers trying to lower the lighted candle into the shell.

Container Molds

Container molds are usually of glass, but the container may be made of anything that won't be damaged by heat. A container candle is burned in its mold. If the mold is a material that is not transparent or translucent, the beauty of the candle is diminished considerably. One of the charms of the glass container is that it permits the soft glow of the candle flame to be visible.

A low melting point wax—125 to 135 degrees—is best for container candles and generally no stearic acid or crystals are used. By using a soft wax with no additives, all the wax will be consumed by the flame so no bits or pieces of wax cling to the inside of container.

A different type of wicking is used for container candles and is called a wire or metal core wick. This is a cloth-covered wire and is much more rigid than the braided wick used in metal molds. The wire is made of a special metal that burns along with its cloth covering.

As there are no holes in a container for threading a wick, other methods are employed to be sure wick remains centered in candle. A small weight may be tied to the end of wick and dropped in place in the bottom of container. This is a makeshift method and if many container candles are planned, a metal wick holder is the answer. This is a small square of metal with slots in the center through which the wick is threaded. It may be fastened to the bottom of the container with a small piece of clay, or even better, pour in enough hot wax to barely cover the wick holder. Allow this wax to harden. Wick is then pulled straight in the center of mold and the end wrapped around a pencil, rod, or other object that is placed across the top of mold. Wick should be centered and remainder of container filled with wax.

Hot wax poured into a cold glass may cause the glass to break, so don't take a chance on it. Warm glass container before pouring. A temperature of around 165 degrees is about right for pouring in glass molds.

Mold should be filled no more than ¾ full and should be refilled when depression forms. A slight depression makes for better burning, so don't refill completely. A water bath is not necessary for container candles. (Illustration No. 2.)

Illustration No. 2. Container candles.

When wax is cold, unwind wick and trim to proper burning length.

Ceramic Molds

Most castings from ceramic molds will be used for decoration rather than for burning and, in this case, there is no need for a wick. If a plaster mold is to be used for a candle, a slight indentation can be scratched in the mold on one side from the bottom of the figure to the bottom of mold. This indentation or ditch will allow a wick to be placed in the mold without causing mold pieces to fit together improperly. A large knot should be tied in the bottom of wick before it is placed in the ditch; then the pieces of the mold fitted together and fastened tightly with a rubber band. Draw wick taut and center it across the top of mold in the same manner as with a metal mold. Clay should be pressed around the knot in the end of the wick to discourage wax leakage.

Plaster molds are made specifically for ceramics because plaster will absorb a great deal of water. When slip or liquid clay is poured into a plaster mold, the water is absorbed by the plaster and the slip becomes damp (but firm) clay. An absorbent mold is the last thing a candlecrafter needs, however, and it is necessary to treat mold to prevent sticking before it is used for wax.

There are two methods in general use for treating molds for wax casting. The first and easiest, is to soak mold in automobile transmission fluid for several hours. When mold has absorbed enough fluid to coat it thoroughly, remove mold from fluid and allow to drain.

Transmission fluid or oil is very lightweight and readily penetrates the plaster. Experiments have shown that of the relatively inexpensive oils available in bulk, this one is the most effective. It will rarely, if ever, be necessary to treat the mold more than once.

With the busy lives most people lead, it is not uncommon for a mold to be placed in oil and then be forgotten for a day or so. Molds left in oil too long will absorb too much oil and castings will be greasy and unfit for use. An effective solution is to run hot water over the mold to remove excess oil.

The second method for treating a mold is to coat the mold cavity with a good grade of varnish or shellac that will withstand high temperatures. Mix together equal parts of turpentine and shellac or varnish and brush this mixture over the entire mold cavity. Let paint dry completely. Continue to apply the varnish and turpentine mixture until mold will absorb no more, allowing each coat to dry between applications. A final coat of pure shellac or varnish may then be applied.

The advantage of this method is a smoother casting because of the slick surface and the fact that mold can be cast at a temperature of 180 degrees. The disadvantage is that the paint will often blur or obscure fine detail in the mold.

If a mold has very little detail, the varnish method is probably best. For figure molds or molds with patterns or designs, stick to the transmission fluid.

Ceramics is a popular hobby and it combines well with candlecrafting. Any candle hobbyist who can make his own holders is the envy of all candlecrafters. If you want to use your molds for ceramics and candlecrafting, there is a way. Oil ruins molds for ceramics and once they've been dunked in transmission oil they aren't much good for anything but wax. Soaking molds in water before pouring wax drastically shortens the life of the mold, but it does allow the use of mold for both ceramics and candles.

Even with the oil treatment, very hot wax may stick to the plaster and it is best to pour ceramic molds at a temperature of about 160 degrees. Let wax cool before trying to separate mold. If pieces will not part easily, put mold in refrigerator for about an hour. If refrigeration doesn't work, soak mold in hot water until wax softens enough to release. Never try to force the opening of plaster molds, as it will be the mold that gives and not the wax.

Many of the plaster molds produce castings of two or more pieces. For example, a casting may have hands, legs, head, etc. that must be attached to complete the figure. To assemble these pieces, dip a small brush in very hot wax and place brush between the two sections to be joined. Press sections together while drawing out the brush. This will leave hot wax between the pieces and weld them together. Joined sections do not always fit together as snugly as they should and there will be a definite joining line showing. These lines can be covered by brushing hot wax the color of casting over the line or seam until the indentation is filled. Any excess wax may be trimmed with a small knife.

Because of the low pouring temperature required for oil-treated molds, the castings have a dull surface when removed from the mold. This dullness can be eliminated by dipping the casting in either untinted wax or wax the color of casting that has been heated to a temperature of 180 to 200 degrees. Dipping should be done after pieces are joined and seam lines trimmed as the hot wax will cover seam lines and make joined pieces adhere better.

Plastic Molds

Wax is prepared in the identical manner as for metal molds, but is poured at a temperature of about 165 degrees. Almost all plastic molds need to be oiled to provide easy mold release and smooth surfaces. Liquid cooking oil applied to the inside surface of a plastic mold with a paper towel makes it much easier to remove candle from mold.

You obviously can't rub the inside of a bottle with an oiled towel and the only thing to do in this case is to pour a small amount of oil in the bottle and shake it vigorously to be certain all inside surfaces are coated. Pour out the oil and save it for use with another mold. Bottle should be turned upside down to allow excess oil to drain.

Any mold performs better if it is warm and this goes for plastic too. Just don't get it so warm that it melts.

So many things are now packaged in plastic bottles and these bottles come in such attractive shapes that it would be a shame not to take advantage of them for candles. Most of these bottles become one-time molds as the candle cannot be pulled from the mold. Mold must be cut and peeled off.

Glass Molds

Container candles are usually poured and burned in glass to permit the light to shine through, but glass containers can also be used as removable molds. Prepare wax in same manner as for metal molds and pour at a temperature of approximately 165 degrees. Mold should be warmed before pouring to reduce the hazard of the glass breaking.

A quick look around the house will unearth many glass containers that would be suitable for candles. On your shelves there will probably be water glasses, pilsner glasses, wine glasses, cups, etc. The openings of these containers are usually large enough to permit removal of the candle by drawing it from the mold.

Empty cosmetic bottles, bath salts bottles, perfume bottles, and many other well-shaped bottles will make lovely candles, but they will not permit the removal of the hardened wax because of small necks or undercuts. These are also one-time molds and must be broken to get the candle out. Wrap glass in a towel to avoid shattered glass scattering over the kitchen and tap the towel with a hammer just hard enough to break the glass. Remove towel and peel off glass fragments.

Wickless Molds

In many of the unorthodox candle molds used, it will be impossible to insert a wick before pouring the candle. Some instances of this would be a bottle with a very thin neck, ball mold where two halves are joined to form a round candle, and some ceramic molds in more than one piece. For candles such as these it is necessary to make a hole in the finished candle for the wick.

If there is a drill around the house, it will be great for drilling a hole in the center of the candle. Another method is to heat an ice pick on your stove burner and gently press it through the center of the candle. The pick may have to be reheated several times during this operation and care must be taken not to force the pick through the wax. If too much force is used, part of the candle may break off.

With some molds, ice pick can be inserted in the wax while it is still in the mold, but before it has hardened completely. After the hole has been made in the candle, dip wick in hot wax, straighten it and place it in the hole. Carefully fill the hole with hot wax after first plugging the hole at the bottom with a piece of clay.

Rubber Molds

If your talents run to sculpturing, you can create original designs for candles or decorations and duplicate these designs many times with rubber molds. The rest of us less talented people can sleuth out unusual figures, antiques, medallions, or even buttons and reproduce them for our candles. The thing to watch for here is the copyright symbol—if it's copyrighted don't make a mold of it.

There are all sorts of liquid rubbers on the market and most of them are not suitable for candle molds. Use only a rubber that will withstand the high heat of the liquid wax. Otherwise, the first pouring will cause the inside of the mold to melt or become tacky. Wax and rubber will stick together, ruining both mold and candle. Most of the candle supply houses have a liquid rubber that is quite compatible with hot wax.

The size of the brushes you will use will depend to a large extent on the size of your mold. Use inexpensive brushes and have at least one soft camel hair and one stiff-bristled brush. If soap or detergent is worked into the bristles of your brushes before you dip them in the rubber, they will be much easier to clean.

If you wish to make a mold of a bas-relief (raised design on one side and flat on the other) simply place the flat side on a smooth, non-porous surface. Fasten the model to the smooth surface with florist's adhesive or rubber cement. Very carefully pour a thin coat of rubber over the model, allowing the rubber to extend beyond the sides of the model about ½″. This extension, or lip, will help you remove the casting when wax is poured into mold.

During the application of the first coat of rubber, great pains must be taken to insure that there are no air bubbles in the rubber. If there are bubbles, prick them with a pin or stab them gently with a stiff bristled brush. Any air holes will be reproduced as bumps in your wax castings.

Allow the first coat to dry until tacky and then brush on as many coats as needed. Let each coat dry to the tack stage before applying more rubber. The number of coats will depend on the size of the model to be covered. A very small object, such as a medallion, would take no more than five coats. A large object might require ten or more coats.

On the larger objects after the first four or five coats have been applied, a filler can be used to make a tougher, thicker mold and thus reduce the number of coats necessary. There are shredded rubbers and plastics that may be mixed with the liquid rubber and brushed on the mold to add thickness and strength. Also, small squares of cheesecloth may be placed over the first few thicknesses of rubber and additional rubber brushed over and worked into the cloth.

The first three coats should be free of air bubbles. After that, have as few bubbles as possible, but on the outer coatings bubbles are not so critical as in the rubber that will form the inner surface of the mold. If desired, the first two or three coats of rubber may be flowed on with a soft brush, working rubber into all cavities. The larger, stiff-bristled brush is better for the top coatings where so much care is not necessary.

Allow rubber to cure for a couple of days before trying to remove model. Placing it in the sun or in a warm—not hot—oven will hasten the drying process. When rubber is dry, remove the model and allow to cure for another 24 hours just to be on the safe side. After that you can start pouring your wax.

Full figure models must be molded in two sections for best results. It is possible to cover the entire figure with rubber and split the mold up the back and remove it. However, when this is done there is always the problem of sealing the split tightly enough to prevent leaking when hot wax is poured into the mold. The two-section mold takes more time but is much more satisfactory in the long run.

To make a two-section mold it is necessary to imbed half the model in a solid substance of some sort. Ceramic clay is my choice for this job, although plastiline or even plaster of paris is sometimes used. If ceramic clay is kept moist it will last indefinitely and its pliability can be increased by the addition of water.

Place the model on a flat surface and add clay to the underside of the model until half of the model is encased in the clay. Smooth the clay around the model and be sure the clay is flush against the sides of the model. Sponge off any bits of clay from the top side of model.

Keys help in fitting the mold together when it is finished. A key may be made by taking a spoon and digging a small hole in the clay alongside the model. Be careful when brushing on the rubber so this hole has only a coating of rubber and is not completely filled. When the second half of the mold is made, this indentation will become a protrusion or bump, and the two will fit together for a perfect alignment of the mold.

When model has been imbedded in clay, cover the exposed half of the model with rubber in the same manner as when making a bas-relief mold. Let mold cure for at least 24 hours and then remove all of the clay from around the model. Clean model so there are no bits of clay sticking to it. You now have a model that is half imbedded in a rubber mold. Leaving the model in the mold, lightly oil the lip of the mold so the new application of rubber will not stick to it. Apply liquid rubber to the exposed half of model, allowing the rubber to extend to the edge of the lip of the half mold that you have already made. After sufficient coats of rubber have been applied to the model, allow mold to dry for two days.

Because of the flexibility and elasticity of rubber, it is necessary to place the mold in a form that will keep it from losing its shape when wax is poured into it. A plaster shell that follows the exact contours of the outside of the mold will keep the mold from stretching or sagging.

Plaster may be obtained at any hobby or ceramic shop in small quantities. However, if you expect to make several rubber molds, buy the 100-pound bag from a lumber yard or hardware store for considerable savings. Ask for molding plaster.

A container for holding the mold and the plaster shell can be almost anything that extends 1″ or so beyond the mold. A well-greased pan or even a cardboard box lined with aluminum foil can serve as your container. Whatever you use, be certain that the inside walls are well greased.

The next step calls for more estimating. Look in your container or box and try to guess how much water it will take to cover half of the mold when it is in the box. Take the estimated amount of water and place it in a pan or bowl. Slowly sift the plaster through your fingers into the water, covering the whole surface of the water and not just the middle of bowl. The saturation point will be reached when plaster forms small peaks above the top of water. Insert your hand in the bowl and gently stir the plaster and water. Stir until plaster is the consistency of heavy cream. Then slowly pour plaster into pan or box and let sit until it begins to harden. When it has reached the stage where it begins to congeal and is no longer liquid, push your mold, which has been well greased with a layer of vaseline, into the plaster. Only the bottom half of the mold should be imbedded in the plaster. Scrape away the plaster that the mold displaced so that top of shell is fairly smooth. Let plaster harden for several hours.

When plaster is hard, grease with vaseline the top surface of the plaster shell you have just made. Also be sure the mold is well greased so it will not stick to the plaster. Roll a cylinder of clay and place it flush against the bottom of your mold. When the clay is removed, you will have a hole through which to pour your wax.

Stir up another batch of plaster and pour it over the mold that is still in the box. Let plaster harden overnight and then remove it from the box or container in which it was poured. Open the two halves carefully as plaster is quite fragile until it is thoroughly dry. It may be necessary to take the blade of a knife and push it gently between the two halves to pry them open.

Remove the rubber mold from the plaster shell and peel it off the model. Let both rubber mold and plaster shell cure for a couple of days before using them.

When you are ready to pour wax into the rubber mold, fit the two pieces together and place in one of the plaster shells. Fit the other shell over the top of the mold and fasten as tightly as possible. Strips cut from bicycle or automobile inner tubes make good heavy-duty rubber bands for holding the halves of the plaster shell together. Pour wax into the hole made by the clay cylinder and refill as necessary. When wax is hard, peel the rubber mold from the casting.

When mixing your plaster, wash your hands and utensils as soon after pouring as possible for ease of cleaning. Go to an outside faucet for this clean-up job as plaster is worse than wax for clogging drains.

Summary

For quick reference, here is a brief summary of the basic steps in making a candle:

Break wax into small pieces with a hammer, place in container and heat slowly.

When wax has melted, add stearic and/or crystals, if desired, and heat to correct temperature.

While wax is melting, insert wick in mold and warm mold.

When wax reaches correct pouring temperature, add color and/or scent and pour wax slowly into tilted mold.

Place mold in water bath and leave until depression forms in top of wax.

Punch holes in wax near the wick and refill with hot wax same color as candle.

Allow candle to cool completely before trying to remove from mold.

Common Problems and Their Solutions

Frost Marks

These are whitish patches on the surface of a candle. They can be minimized by polishing briskly with a soft cloth. Frost marks are often caused by wax not being hot enough when poured and mold not being warm at time of pouring.

Pit Marks

Wax poured into a mold too rapidly causes splashing and the splashing creates air bubbles. When the bubbles burst they leave little holes on the surface of the candle. Lint or dust in a mold can also cause this condition.

Internal Fractures

This is caused by too rapid cooling of wax or by refilling after wax has hardened.

Candle Hard to Release from Mold

Inferior wax is often responsible for this problem. Dents in metal molds or any mold with undercuts or a larger body than opening can make it almost impossible to remove candle. If wax is poured over the top of candle when refilling and allowed to run between candle and sides of mold, it will prohibit mold release.

Bubbles Around Bottom of Candle

Bubble lines usually occur if additional water is added after mold has been placed in water bath.

Cave-ins

Holes were not poked in candle soon enough and the vacuum created by cooling wax resulted in caved-in sides.

Mottling

Mottling can be caused by cooling the candle too slowly and usually happens in the summer. Wax that has been remelted several times will be mottled. Almost all wax is mottled to some degree when it is purchased. The addition of stearic acid reduces the transparency of the wax and helps eliminate the mottled appearance.

3

THE INS AND OUTS OF DECORATING

LIFE holds few pleasures more gratifying than to sit back, take a hard, critical look at your finished work, and say to yourself, "I made that and it's good."

Your first efforts at candle decorating should be directed to what pleases you. The likes and dislikes of other people become of prime importance if and when you decide to become a business, but until you do, your satisfaction is all that matters.

This doesn't imply that you should be content with slipshod work; excellent workmanship is within the reach of everyone and has nothing to do with talent, imagination, or creativity. Being able to afford the best is a universal wish and this is one area where the best is obtainable. In all probability, you can make a finer candle than you could buy, even with unlimited money to spend. Many candles I have made for myself or friends couldn't be considered commercially as the time involved would have made the price prohibitive.

Watching a sleek, satiny, unblemished candle slide form a mold is pure pleasure, but what goes on afterward determines whether you have just another candle or an original creation. After you have spent some time working with candles and studying the work of others, you will find it is often possible to name the designer of certain candles. Each person eventually develops a style that is uniquely his own. Even using the same idea, it is unlikely that two people would create identical candles.

For those first, uncertain steps into this new craft, copy freely. The pictures and instructions in this book were put there so you could copy them, step-by-step, if you wish. In the beginning, mastering some of the basic techniques is more important than being original or creative. As you become more surefooted, branch out and be as different as you dare. Above all, don't be afraid to try something new even if you are doubtful about the results. I could fill a large room with discarded candles if all my failures had been kept instead of winding up back in the melting pot.

A decorating file can be a candlecrafter's best friend. Newspapers, magazines, old books, and store windows are all grist for the candlemaker's idea mill. Paper, pencil, and scissors are three of the handiest tools you can have. If the idea is already on paper, cut it out and file it. If it's not on paper, use the pencil to get it there and into the file it goes. Add a pencil and small notebook as part of the standard equipment in your purse so that when an idea comes you can get it down in writing before it slips away. Next time the old imagination gets lazy, the material in your file can be a powerful prodder.

Decoration for some candles can be added while the candle is being poured and the decoration becomes a part of the candle. For want of a better term, we'll call this internal decorating.

Chunk Candles

One of the most common but most attractive examples of internal decorating is the chunk, or marbelized, candle. Candle is made by dropping colored chunks of wax into the mold and filling mold with clear wax. The wick is strung in mold as usual before the chunks are put in. Results may be varied greatly by the size of the wax pieces. Very small chunks will melt more rapidly, thereby producing a greater distribution of color throughout the candle. Larger chunks have less tendency to melt and the candle will have a streaked or marbleized appearance.

Wax cubes may be all one color or several harmonizing colors may be used. If a combination of colors is desired, be sure they are colors that will blend well when they melt. Otherwise candle will have a muddy look where two or more colors merge.

The effects you achieve by using this method will depend to a great extent on the temperature of your clear wax when it is poured into the mold and the melting point of the wax chunks used. Wax poured at about 240 degrees will produce a blending of colors as shown in Illustration No. 3. Wax poured at a lower temperature will cause less melting of the colored chunks and therefore less mingling of colors.

If a hard wax is used for the chunks, any colors may be mixed as they will not be melted by the hot wax and colors will not run together. (Illustration No. 3.)

Illustration No. 3. Candles made by using wax chunks and dye for internal decorating.

Hard and fast rules for making these candles are not possible as the temperature of the pouring wax affects the final outcome and so does the melting point of wax cubes used. Experimenting and keeping records of the results obtained using various waxes and temperatures is the only way to be sure of getting the exact effect desired.

Unless hard wax chunks are used, you will probably find that your wax cubes settle as the hot wax is poured over them. So have a few extra chunks handy to fill in at the top of candle as wax is being poured.

Melting the exact amount of wax for a candle is a rare accomplishment and usually there is wax left over. When this happens, pour leftover wax in a cake pan. When it is firm but not hard, cut it with a knife as you would a pan of fudge. After wax hardens, remove from pan, place the squares in a plastic bag to keep them clean, and you will have chunks all ready for your next candle.

Ice Cube Candle

One of the first things a candlecrafter learns is that wax and water don't mix. A novel exception is the ice cube candle. Instead of wicking mold as is usually done when pouring a candle, dip the wick of a slender candle (a taper from the store will be satisfactory) in hot wax. Turn candle upside down and insert stiffened wick in hole in bottom of mold. Fasten wick to bottom of mold with clay or tape, making sure the wick hole is well sealed to prevent wax leakage. Break ice cubes into small pieces and pack them into mold around the candle, positioning cubes so candle is kept in center of mold. After filling mold with ice, pour out any accumulated water. Wax heated to a temperature of approximately 240 degrees should be used for pouring. After pouring, mold should be immersed in water bath but refilling is not necessary. Pour water from mold and remove candle when wax hardens. (Illustration No. 4.)

Vary the appearance of these candles with different sizes of ice. The smaller the ice pieces, the lighter and lacier your candle. Try the small marble-sized ice balls or the larger balls that can be made in your refrigerator in special trays if you get tired of the regular ice cubes and pieces of ice.

Instead of a plain taper, buy one of the candles made especially to drip in colors. Put the ice cubes in mold as usual and use a hard wax for pouring. When lighted, wax from the taper will drip in colors and seep through the holes made by the melted ice.

The holes made by the ice may be sprayed with glitter glue and covered with tiny glass beads for a frosted look. Some people pour or brush hot wax of a different color in the ice holes. Wax flowers are also sometimes placed in the holes.

Decorating With Dye

The primary function of a candle dye is to uniformly color wax, but it performs well as a decorating medium also. Pour candle as usual but do not add any color to the wax. Just before

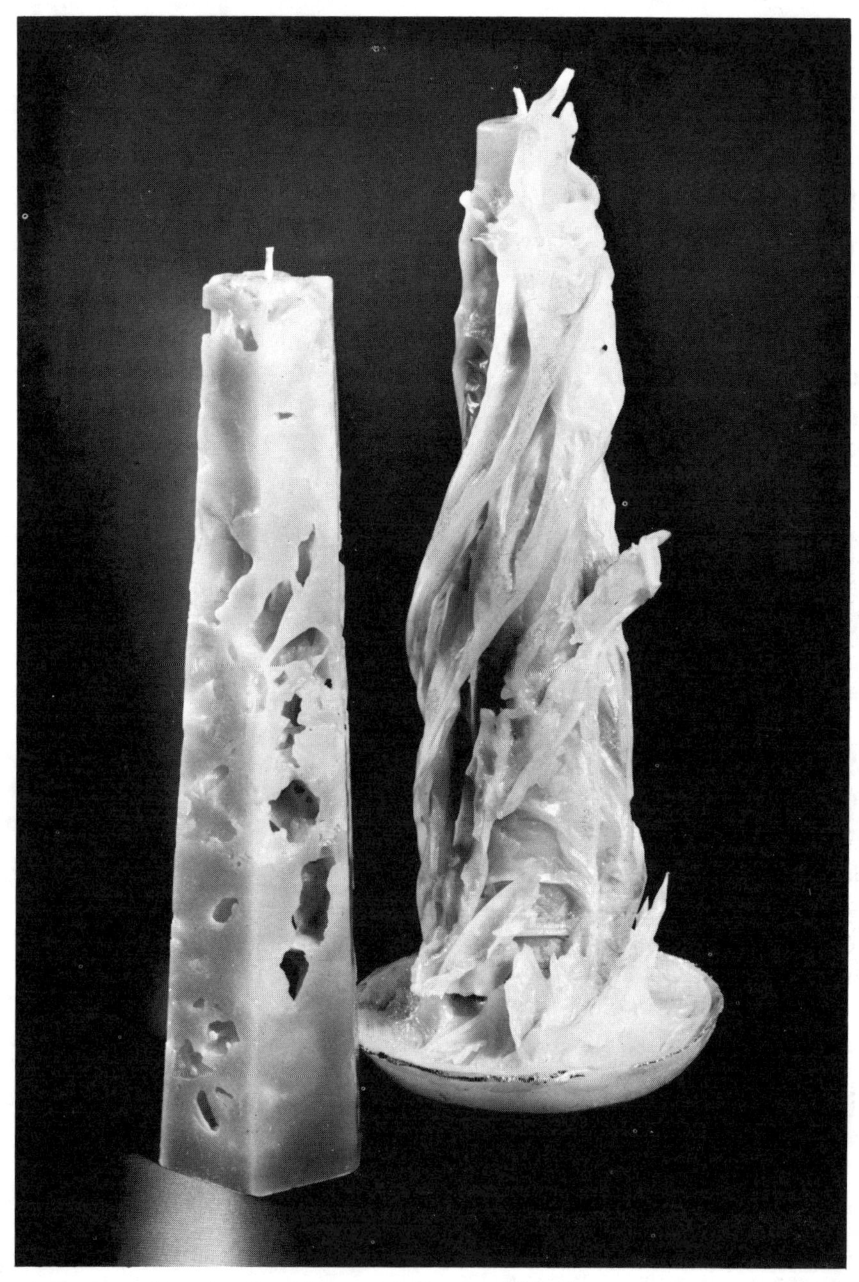

Illustration No. 4. Ice Cube and Fantasy Candle.

putting candle in water bath, drop a few grains of powdered dye around the inside edge of mold. As the dye sinks to the bottom of mold, it will leave thin colored streaks in the wax along the side of candle. Again, be careful when you mix your colors to be sure they will blend well. For example, red and yellow will blend into orange, blue and red become purple, and blue and yellow produce green. (Illustration No. 3.)

Wider streaks may be obtained by dropping very small pieces of dye buds around the inside of mold instead of powdered dye.

Imbedding

If you want to mystify your friends, try imbedding wax arrangements in your candles. Like much of candlecrafting, this looks extremely complicated, but is really quite simple. From a money angle, this can be one of the most profitable of all candles and it has the added advantage of being sturdy enough to ship well. I have seen candles of this type in shops priced from $10 to $30 for rather elementary designs. One of my candlemaking friends reported seeing a very large and elaborate mosaic tile candle during her travels that was priced at $600.

A few exceptional people can follow through the glimmer of an idea to a completely jelled plan in their heads. If you are one of these people, skip the next few sentences. If you're one of us ordinary mortals, it's best to plan your design on paper.

There are countless design books in the public library and drawings from these books can be copied or used for inspiration. Any imbedments must be one dimensional, and if figures are to be used they should be of the silhouette type. Wax tiles can be cut in different sizes and laid out to form mosiacs.

After you have drawn your pattern on paper, cut it out with scissors or a razor blade. Pour very hard wax to a depth of about ¼″ in a pan that has been well oiled or lined with waxed paper. When wax is firm, place paper pattern over the wax and cut around it with a sharp knife. Remove wax design and place it on a sheet of saran wrap. Glue design to saran wrap with rubber cement and let sit until cement has hardened enough to hold wax securely.

If wax design is to be used with a round candle, it must be

pliable enough to fit the curve of the candle without breaking. Wax can be warmed sufficiently by leaving it in the sun for a short time or by placing it between two sheets of waxed paper and folding a heating pad turned to low over the wax.

Lower the sheet of saran wrap into the mold with wax pieces toward the outside. Always keep in mind during this operation that the bottom of the mold will be the top of the candle when it is removed and position your design accordingly. Saran wrap should be long enough so a piece may be folded over the edge of mold and taped to outside. If the mold is large enough, insert your hand and gently press the wax design against side of mold. For a small mold, use a knife handle to press design against side of mold. Design must fit as snugly as possible against mold wall so hot wax will not run between decoration and side of mold.

Fill mold with small cubes or chunks of wax, packing chunks as tightly as possible to hold design in place. When wax chunks are packed to within about 1″ of top of mold, remove saran wrap from side of mold and cut it off level with the wax chunks. Continue filling mold with chunks until mold is full. Heat wax the same color as chunks to 200 degrees and pour into mold. Wax may be poured over the chunks in center of mold or down the side of mold opposite the design. Don't tilt the mold and pour down the side holding design, as seen in Illustration No. 3.

Place mold in water bath after filling.

Saran wrap will melt rather than burn if it should come in contact with the flame and its transparency makes it undetectible in the candle. After candle is removed from mold, trim and level it as usual.

Use a hard wax at least ¼″ thick for design so edges will stay clean and sharp with no blurring.

Occasionally these candles will come from the mold with surface blemishes. If there is a hole caused by pouring wax not completely surrounding a wax chunk, fill in the hole by brushing in hot wax same color as candle. A hot wax dip will effectively conceal any repair work or minor imperfections.

Another candlecrafting trick is to lightly pass the flame of a liquid petroleum torch over the surface of the candle. These L.P. torches are inexpensive and are stocked by most hardware and automotive supply stores.

Fantasy Candle

The fantasy candle is well named as it is most unusual. Almost any poured candle with a diameter of from 1″ to 3″ may be used. Place the candle in a bowl about 5″ or 6″ in diameter and pour hot wax into the bowl to a depth of about ½″. Candle will be held in place by the hardened wax. When wax in bowl is cool, heat additional wax to a temperature of 165 degrees and pour in another inch or so of hot wax. Holding candle near the top, immediately lower it and the bowl into a container of tepid water.

Container should be tall enough so candle will be completely covered by water. The liquid wax will rise and cling to side of candle as it is submerged. Wear gloves when dunking candle to protect hands from hot wax.

When wax is cold, remove candle from bowl. You will find that candle has a built-in, bowl-shaped base and this base can be left as is, textured, or sprinkled with glitter. (Illustration No. 4.)

The big drawback to the fantasy candle is that it's extremely fragile. A very hard wax used for the bowl pouring will partially solve this problem.

Layered Candles

Candles to rival the rainbow are possible with this simple technique. A layer of wax as deep or shallow as you wish is poured into mold and allowed to get absolutely cold. Another layer is poured on top of the first one, letting this layer harden before pouring again. This process is repeated until the mold is filled. Wax should be heated to approximately 180 degrees for pouring.

Your color choice is unlimited. Two colors may be alternated or a different color poured for each layer. Monochrome candles consisting of different shades of one color can be very beautiful. Start with a dark shade for the first layer and progressively lighten each pouring. Or you can reverse the procedure and begin with a light shade that becomes deeper with each layer.

As colorful as these candles are, they need no further decoration. If decoration is used, be sparing. An example might be a Fourth of July candle poured in red, white, and blue with a few sequin stars scattered over the blue field. Too much ornamentation would detract from the total effect of the candle.

By permitting wax to harden between each pouring, you will have a sharp division between colors. Sometimes it is preferable for the dividing lines between the shades to be less clear-cut and, in this case, wait only until a thick film has formed. Pour additional wax at about 200 degrees and layers will have a blurred, fuzzy appearance. Be careful about your colors so the blended areas will not be muddy.

Layers may be angled by tilting mold before pouring and holding in position with props of some sort. After each pouring has hardened, raise the mold a little. During the last pouring the mold should be in a vertical position.

By tilting the mold first to one side and then the other, the colors, or layers, may be alternated. During the first pouring tilt mold and support it the same as is done with angled colors. For the second pouring, position your supports so the mold rests on the opposite side. Keep alternating position of mold, raising it a little with each pouring. Last pouring should be done with mold standing straight.

An example of alternating layers is shown in Illustration No. 5. A soda glass was used for a mold and layers of red (strawberry) and white (vanilla) were poured. White whipped wax was used to simulate whipped cream and before wax hardened two short straws were inserted near the edge of the glass. A ball of red wax half buried in the whipped wax made a convincing cherry.

Stalagmite Candle

Each stalagmite candle will be an original. Regardless of how hard you tried, it would be impossible to make two exactly alike.

Your mold can be almost any large bottle or can with straight sides. Diameter of the mold should be at least 4″ so heat from votive candle will not melt the wax shell. Stalagmite candle in Illustration No. 5 was molded around a milk bottle.

Mold should be several inches above table top when candle is poured so drips will not be stopped abruptly by the table. When using a jar or bottle with a small neck for a mold, turn mold

Illustration No. 5. Layered Candle and Stalagmite Candle.

upside down and place neck of bottle in a heavy drinking glass. One of your metal candle molds can be used for elevating a wide-mouth jar. Place stand and mold in cake pan so wax won't run all over the table. Coat mold with a thin film of cooking oil.

Melt wax and let cool until a thin film forms over the top. Slowly pour wax over the bottom of mold so it runs and drips down the sides. Wax must be reheated and then cooled between each pouring. Continue pouring until a shell of sufficient thickness is formed.

Scrape wax build-up off the bottom of mold between pourings so candle will have a level surface. While wax is still warm, cut a circle in bottom of shell to fit over votive candle.

Two or more colors may be used and they may be alternated between pourings or one color may be poured and final coatings made with another color.

The stalagmite candle derives much of its appeal from its rough and rugged exterior. It can be smoothed, if desired, by pouring a final coating of hot wax over the whole thing.

Contraction of the cooling wax will cause shell to cling to the mold. It may be possible to slide shell from the greased mold without any trouble, but, if not, fill mold with hot water for a few seconds and shell will slip off easily. Hot water should be left in mold just long enough to soften inside coating of wax for easy removal. Don't let it stand in mold long enough to melt the sides of shell.

Two-Toned Candle

A glass container or metal mold works equally well with this candle. Pour in usual manner and leave in water bath until a thin shell forms. Pour out the liquid wax as you would if making a hurricane candle. Allow shell to cool and fill the cavity with wax of a different color.

Normally, the second pouring of wax should be made in the center of mold rather than down the side to avoid melting wax on side of mold. However, hot wax can be directed in such a manner that portions of the shell will melt and patches of the colored inner layer will be part of the surface of the candle.

If portions of the inside of wax shell are scraped off, the thin film of wax remaining will melt when it comes in contact with hot wax. Wax shell should not be cooled before second pouring if color patches are desired as warm wax will melt more readily than cold wax.

Surface Decoration

Attaching decoration to the outside of candles presents some problems. So far, no glue on the market is completely satisfactory for fastening heavy objects to wax, but paper, small jewels, sequins, etc. will stick with no trouble.

Glue is occasionally the only possible agent to use for attaching a specific ornament and there is a method that will make it more effective when used on wax. Scratch the surface of candle where decoration is to be attached and spread glue on the roughened area. Add a wisp of cotton to the glued area. Put glue on the ornament and press against the candle where cotton has been added.

The person who invents a glue specifically for wax will be able to sell it to candlecrafters by the gallons, but until then, there are other attaching methods that are quite successful.

If the production of straight pins were suddenly halted, many candlecrafters would panic. Pins are the basic, and for some the only, fastening agents. A variety of objects can be attached to candles by using these slivers of steel.

The candle on the left in Illustration No. 6 demonstrates the pin technique. All of the decorations are of gold metallic foil and all are attached with gold sequin pins. The pins are placed in the outside edges of the foil and pushed into the wax. The end of the handle of an X-acto knife makes a good tool for pressing pins into wax and saves wear and tear on the fingers. A thimble also performs this task quite efficiently.

Silver foil is not used as extensively as gold, but when there is a need for it, sometimes it is possible to avoid buying silver if you already have gold foil. Many of the gold foils have a silver base. A small piece of cotton dipped in acetone (from the drugstore) and rubbed lightly over the gold will reveal the silver lining. This doesn't work on all golds, but do try it before you make a trip to the store for some silver foil. Needless to say, silver foil should be fastened to candles with silver sequin pins.

Candle on the right in Illustration No. 6 is another example

Illustration No. 6. Candles using pin technique.

of the pin technique, this time using metallic foil and artificial foliage. Sequin pins were the fasteners for the foil and regular straight pins were used for the plants. Straight pins are sturdier and will hold the heavier decorations more securely than the smaller sequin pins. Pins were inserted through the stems of the cattails and through the stems of the bubble branches, with the bubble branches arranged so the pins in cattail stems were hidden.

Naked pin heads on a candle are sloppy and unprofessional, so try to hide them. It's not always possible to arrange everything so that each pinhead is covered, but they can be camouflaged with paint or a drop of hot wax the same color as the decoration.

Grapes on the candle on right in Illustration No. 7 were also put on with pins. Some of the plastic grapes were lifted while the pins were pushed through the stems. When the grapes were dropped, the pins became invisible.

Even with this small group of candles, it is evident that with some pins and a few materials, very attractive candles can be quickly and easily made. Many of the expensive candles you see in the candle shops are decorated in a matter of minutes with an artificial flower or two and straight pins. In these shops candles costing less than $1.00 to make will readily sell for $5.00 or more.

Artificial Flowers

Artificial flowers may also be fastened by pinning the stems to candle. This method is fine if you wish the sides of the flowers to rest against the candle. But what if you want the back of the flower to fit flush against the candle surface? Pins aren't much help in this instance, but there is an easy way.

Hold flower against candle to get the exact position you want and with a knife dig out a small hole in the wax where stem will fit. Place the point of an icepick over the burner of your stove and leave it till it is red hot. Cut flower stem so it is no longer than ½″. Push the hot icepick into hole in candle and immediately insert flower stem into this hole. Candle should be placed on its side during this operation so melted wax created by the hot pick will not run down side of candle. Melted wax will harden around flower stem and the flower is there to stay. (Illustration No. 7.)

Illustration No. 7. Flowers fastened to candle with ice pick, and grapes attached with pins.

The reason for scooping a small amount of wax from the side of candle is to prevent the wax displaced by the hot icepick from overflowing and running down candle.

Any number of flowers may be fastened to a candle in this manner. If leaves are to be used as part of the decoration, they should be pinned in place before flower stems are inserted.

Whipped Wax

In all likelihood the favorite decorating aid of candle-crafters is whipped wax. In addition to adding to the attractiveness of a candle, it covers flaws and blemishes so no one ever suspects they are there. Another duty whipped wax performs is attaching decorations that are not too heavy.

Whipped wax is exactly what the name implies—wax that has been whipped with a fork or an egg beater. Whipping creates a light frothy wax that greatly resembles snow. Beating with a fork produces a rather coarse effect, while the beater-whipped wax is much finer in texture.

A metal mixing bowl is the best utensil for whipping wax but is not essential. In the metal bowl the wax can be heated and reheated without the bother of melting in one container and then pouring into another for beating. Changing colors is facilitated when the metal bowl is used. Hardened wax in bowl can be melted poured out, and another color added. However, any bowl or pan can be used that is deep enough to keep the wax splatters inside container while wax is beaten.

One of the additional charms of whipped wax is that it is so simple to make. Melt your wax, let it cool until a film forms over the top and then beat until wax is fluffy. Whipped wax will adhere to candle better if it is not beaten until it is dry. Whip wax just until a heavy coating of froth forms. Scoop wax off the top of the still-liquid wax in bottom of bowl and apply to candle with a fork or spoon. Keep whipping the wax and removing top layer until wax hardens.

The addition of stearic acid to the hot wax will make your snow really white. Add color to the wax just before removing pan from the stove. Pastel colors in whipped wax are prettier than dark ones, as whipping seems to dull brilliant colors. There is nothing more nauseating than red whipped wax.

Wax may be applied to candle with a knife, fork, or spoon. It is often "dumped" onto the candle, especially for snow scenes. After wax is applied to candle and has cooled slightly, it can be pressed lightly with the back of a spoon or fork for unusual effects.

Glitter and whipped wax seem to be made for each other. Glitter can be sprinkled on the warm whipped wax just after it has been put on a candle and no glue is necessary to hold it. To apply glitter after wax hardens, spray glitter cement over the wax and sprinkle on glitter.

A jar with a shaker top will distribute glitter evenly over a large area. For more control when making a glitter design, try using a doll-sized baby bottle. Cut a small hole in the end of the nipple. This hole will release a small stream of glitter that can be placed exactly as you want it.

Illustration No. 8 shows white whipped wax placed on a candle, a plastic nativity scene pressed into the wax, and mica flakes added for highlight.

Place candle on its side when applying whipped wax. If candle is in a vertical position, wax tends to slide off the slick surface. More sticking power is provided if candle surface is roughened slightly before putting on wax.

The pushing of an object into whipped wax will often displace some of the still-liquid wax, causing it to run down the side of candle. These runs, or drips, can be quickly removed by letting the wax cool slightly and then flicking off with a fingertip. The whitish line sometimes left by these drips can be eliminated by rubbing the spot with a soft cloth.

Wax Decorations

Decorations made of wax are usually fastened by two methods. One is to place the decoration against candle and with a small brush apply hot wax the same color as candle around and under the decoration. Be as professional as possible with this method and make the wax brushings as invisible and inconspicuous as you can.

Another technique involves the heated icepick, this time with wire. Punch two holes in decoration with hot icepick and immediately insert two short pieces of wire. The wire should

Illustration No. 8. Candles decorated with wax grapes and leaves, whipped wax and nativity scene, and sealing wax.

protrude from decoration about ½″. Let wax solidify around the wire and then press wire against candle to mark the spots where they will be inserted. Again use the hot icepick on the candle to make two holes and place the ends of the wire in these holes.

The leaves in Illustration No. 8 were attached to candle with brushed-wax method and the heavier grapes were put on with wires. Plastic figurines, etc. may be attached by drilling small holes in their backs, gluing the wire in holes, and then fastening to candle.

A small soldering iron or wood-burning tool will very effectively weld decorations to a candle. This is tricky and practice is needed to get the hang of it. The tip of the tool is run between decoration and candle, melting the wax on both and sealing the two together. It is necessary to work fast when using these tools to avoid melting an excess amount of wax.

Sealing Wax

One of the least used candle decorating aids is sealing wax. The reason for this is because it's also one of the hardest to master. Simple patterns such as that shown in Illustration No. 8 can be done on the first try. More complicated designs, blending and shading, require considerable practice, but the results are well worth the effort involved.

This wax is made in a multitude of colors, including the metallics, and is available in a solid stick form or with a wick in the center. When using sealing wax with a wick, the wax is melted by the heat from the wick flame. It is necessary to use an alcohol lamp to melt the solid stick type. The wick method is better for the beginner, but the alcohol method is usually preferred by the professional.

The beginning point, when applying sealing wax to a candle, is always a small dot of wax. This dot acts as an anchor and prevents the wax from sliding around on candle as the design is put on. Dot is put on candle by lightly touching the melted wax on the end of the stick to the candle.

To make a design such as the one illustrated, place your dot at the bottom of candle and then gradually drip the sealing wax in a curving line toward the top. Branches added on the side are started at the main branch and dribbled outward.

Beautiful flowers can be made with sealing wax and they are much more durable than those made with ordinary wax. Use a very lightweight cardboard or tagboard and cut the number of petals and leaves needed for your flowers. Coat one side of the petals with sealing wax, being careful to extend the wax to the edges. Turn petals over and cover the other side with the wax. Sealing wax hardens quickly and it is necessary to work fast with long, sweeping strokes. While wax is still warm, with the pointed end of an orange stick or ball point pen, make veins in the leaves and flowers. If wax hardens before all this can be accomplished, grasp tip of petal with pliers and hold over an open flame for a few seconds. Wax will soften enough to be easy to work with.

Sculpturing Wax

Sculpturing wax, sometimes called modeling wax or plastic wax, is just what the name indicates. It is a soft wax extremely unsuitable for making candles, but perfect for modeling your own decorations. It's also an expensive wax, but well worth the expense. Scattered through this book you will find some of the many ways in which this versatile wax may be used to enhance your candles.

Sculpturing wax, when cold, is hard and unworkable, but it can be warmed easily. It may be melted and allowed to sit until cool enough to handle. If only a small amount is needed, place it in a pan of warm water for about fifteen minutes. You can even combine your sculpturing wax and your sunbathing. On a hot summer day the heat from the sun is sufficient to make your wax pliable in minutes.

The one big disadvantage of this low melting point wax is that it's inclined to droop on a sweltering summer day. The addition of stearic or crystals will greatly improve its heat resistant qualities. Only a small amount is needed—too much will affect the plastic quality of the wax. Regular candle wax may also be added up to ½ of the total amount of wax.

Usually, the first thing the novice wants to make from

sculpturing wax is a flower. This is easier to do if the wax is in a sheet rather than a solid block. Wax sheets are made by heating wax and pouring a thin layer on a flat surface.

This surface may be many things and each candlecrafter has his favorite. Some use teflon cookie sheets—others a pane of oiled glass. An oil-soaked slab of plaster, or plaster bat, is excellent for this purpose. My preference is a sheet of waxed paper. Spread a sheet of waxed paper on a table and pour wax on the paper. Wax should cool slightly before it is poured on the paper, as very hot wax will melt the wax on the paper and stick. Let the wax sheet cool until it is firm, cut out your design and peel off the waxed paper.

A warm surface will keep your wax pliable while you are working. A simple contraption extensively used by candlecrafters for keeping wax soft is a box without the top. A hole is cut in the side of box and a light cord and socket inserted in hole. Put a light bulb in the socket and place a pane of glass over the top of box. Enough heat will be generated by the light bulb to heat the glass and keep the wax warm.

Another way to keep wax soft while you are working with it is to place it on waxed paper and put the paper on a heating pad turned low.

Besides its usefulness for decorating, sculpturing wax is much better for attaching decorations than the ordinary candle wax. High melting point waxes become extremely hard and brittle in cold weather and when hard, have a slick surface. Sculpturing wax, on the other hand, is quite sticky and does not become brittle when the temperature drops.

Press Molds

Press molds are plaster molds made for ceramics but adopted by the candlecrafter. These molds produce castings that are flat on one side and have a raised design on the other. Wax may be poured or pressed into these molds. Pressing is recommended because it is much faster. A dozen pressings can be made while you are waiting for wax to cool enough to remove one casting made by pouring.

To use the press molds, merely push a small piece of soft sculpturing wax into the mold cavity and press down an all sides. Hold your thumb over the wax in the cavity and run a knife between thumb and top of mold. Use a dull knife or you might slice off a bit of your thumb. Pressure from your thumb will keep wax from pulling out of the cavity while excess is being trimmed. Insert tip of knife just inside the mold cavity and remove casting. While casting is still pliable, place it on candle and shape to fit.

Casting can be fastened to candle by putting a drop of hot sculpturing wax between casting and candle and pressing the two together.

Castings from a flower and leaf press mold were used for decorating the taper on right in Illustration No. 9.

Wax Flowers

A separate book could—and should—be written to give all the information needed for making the many and varied kinds of flowers appropriate for decorating candles.

Wax flowers are considered by some candlecrafters to be the ultimate in candle decoration. Skilled and practiced hands can mold flowers that sometimes surpass Mother Nature's. Do use nature's handiwork for your model though. Take a flower apart—petal by petal, if necessary—and study its shape and formation. Poinsettia petals are almost straight, the center portion of a daffodil is ruffled, and the petals of a rose are curled. When fresh flowers aren't available for study, use some of the real-looking plastic ones.

Real flowers can't be copied exactly as we have limitations that don't apply to nature. Get the feel of a particular flower and adapt it to wax. An example of such an adaption is shown on the left in Illustration No. 9.

To make the center of the rose, cut a thin strip of wax, approximately 1½″ long. Begin at one end and roll this strip rather loosely, curving the top edge outward as strip is rolled. Four sets of petals were made using the pattern in Illustration No. 10. A thin sheet of wax was poured, pattern placed over wax, and petals cut with a knife. The outer edges of the petals were pinched for a thin, natural look and were then rolled and curled backward. Each petal was cupped by pressing slightly with the thumb.

The four sets of petals were stacked one on top of the other and fastened together with hot wax. Rolled center was placed

Illustration No. 9. Hand-molded wax rose and taper with press mold decorations.

Illustration No. 10. Pattern for rose petals. Cut at least three sets.

in middle of top set of petals and also attached with hot wax. Individual petals were then gently pushed into desired positions. (Illustration No. 11.)

Another, and more widely used, method of making a rose is to roll the center in the same manner as above. Small balls of wax are pressed into petal shapes and each petal is attached around the center. Petals are added until rose is as full as desired. Very acceptable roses can be made in this way, but you wind up with an excess amount of wax at the bottom of the flower that has to be cut off so rose can be fastened to candle. Also considerably more time is involved in making a rose in this fashion.

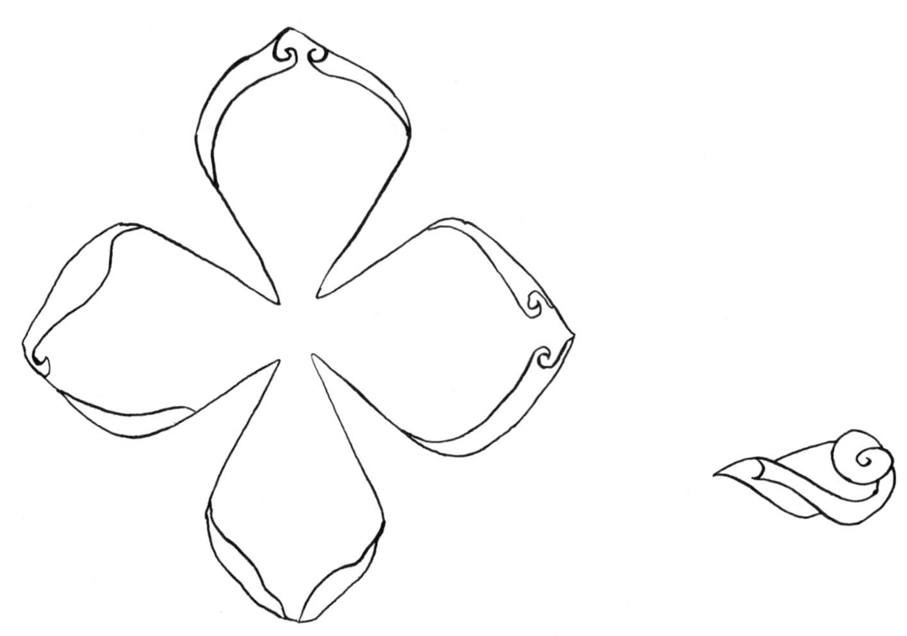

Illustration No. 11. Rolled center of rose and back view of petal section when edges are rolled.

The public library usually has a book or two with patterns for making paper flowers. Often these designs and instructions can be adapted for making wax flowers.

Wax Drapes

The wax spiral on left in Illustration No. 12 is in reality an elongated triangle of wax. Measure candle and cut a paper pattern to avoid having triangle too long or too short. Fold the botton of triangle around candle about an inch from candle bottom. Wind the rest of triangle around candle. Use hot wax to fasten spiral to candle and then dip bottom portion of candle in hot wax. This dipping will soften the sculpturing wax on lower portion of candle and it can be pressed with the fingers to eliminate any raw edges. Brush glue along sides of spiral and add glitter.

Decoration for the other candle in Illustration No. 12 was also cut in a triangular shape. Lower portion of triangle was wrapped around candle as was done with the spiral. The top

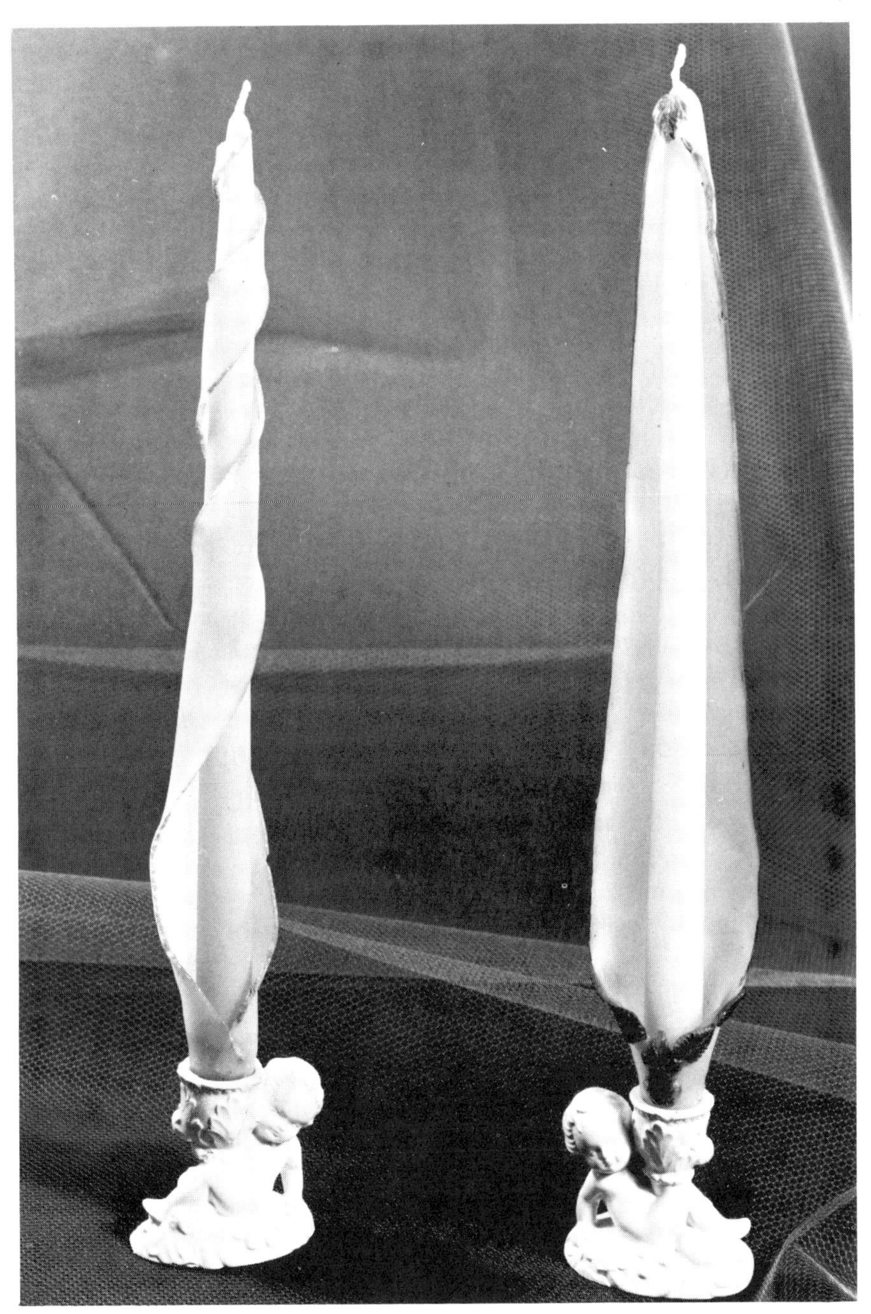

Illustration No. 12. Sculptured Wax Decorations.

tip of the triangle was snipped off and triangle top then folded around upper portion of candle. One small wax leaf was placed at the top of taper to cover joining line and six small leaves were attached near bottom for the same purpose.

The Cover-up

There may be a candlecrafter who always pours a perfect candle—but I doubt it. Even the most experienced has a goof-up sometimes. If the candle is absolutely impossible, it can be thrown back in the pot, remelted, and poured again. That is one of the bonuses of candlecrafting—even with a complete failure you haven't lost anything but your time, as most of the materials can be reused.

Sometimes a candle will have a few pit or pock marks. Illustration No. 13 shows how scattered flaws can be covered with sequins so no one will ever suspect. A definite pattern can be worked out or the sequins can give the impression of having been put on at random. Sequins may be glued or pinned in place.

Regardless of the careful precautions taken, water will occasionally seep into the mold through wick hole and the top of your candle will resemble a piece of swiss cheese. Remove candle from mold and drain off any water trapped inside the wax. Fill the hole or holes with hot wax. Cover top of candle with whipped wax, extending it down the sides. Warm wax can be poured over the top of candle and allowed to drip down the sides. This not only covers up all the holes but is quite attractive. Glitter can be sprinkled on while wax is warm or gold paint touched to the raised portions. (Right candle in Illustration No. 13.)

Whipped wax is famous as a cover-upper. Less extensive coverage may be obtained by heating wax in a container as tall as your candle. Let wax cool till a film forms and beat until you have a layer of whipped wax an inch or two thick. Dip candle into the wax and when it is withdrawn, it will be flecked with whipped wax but not solidly covered.

Texturing can be used to good advantage when you have a candle that's less than perfect. Melt wax, let cool, and beat until a thin foam forms. Crumple a piece of paper (paper towels are good for this) into a wad and dip into the foam. Press the wax-

Illustration No. 13. Sequin and whipped wax cover-ups.

covered paper lightly against candle. When paper is removed it will leave scattered peaks and ridges of wax on the candle surface. Texturing can be done in one color or several colors may be used for variety and interest.

The round hurricane on the left in Illustration No. 14 was made by pouring wax into a bowl and pouring out the liquid wax when a thin shell had formed. Two halves were poured in this manner and then joined together with hot wax. A small hole was cut in the bottom for a votive candle and a large hole cut in the top. Texturing was employed to cover the joining lines and peaks were touched with gold paint for added emphasis.

An accident led to the method of decorating other candle in Illustration No. 14. A wax-filled mold tipped over as it was being lowered into the water bath and the contours of the warm wax as it came in contact with the water fascinated me. I began pouring hot sculpturing wax into warm water and found endless patterns could be achieved. The results are entirely different depending on the heat of the wax, heat of the water, and the distance of wax from the water when it is poured.

As soon as wax is cool enough to handle, take it out of the water and wrap it around a disfigured candle and trim off any excess.

Dipping

There are at least three times when dipping can be used to good advantage. One is to put another coat of wax over minor surface flaws; another is to change or deepen the color of a candle; the third is to get a tight seal between candle and decoration.

Wax for most dipping purposes should be heated to approximately 240 degrees. A dipping vat taller than the candle and at least two inches wider is necessary for successful dipping. Two large coffee cans soldered together make an adequate container or a sheet metal shop can make one to any specifications. The candle supply houses also stock these items.

Hold candle by wick and lower it slowly into the melted wax. Candle should be dipped just to the top edge. If it is completely submerged, the wax running off the top of candle will cause unsightly drips when candle is withdrawn. Leave candle

Illustration No. 14. Textured bowl hurricane and wax-covered candle.

in hot wax for several seconds or for a slow count of six. This will permit a good bond between the wax coating and candle surface. If this bond is not obtained, coating may pull away from candle in spots, causing raised areas or blisters. If possible, let candles cure for several days before dipping them.

Temperature of wax to be used for adding color should be about 200 degrees. Several dippings may be necessary to obtain the desired depth of color. Shading is possible by dipping only a portion of the candle each time. Suppose you are using a dark red dipping wax. Dip the first couple of inches of candle and withdraw. Allow wax to cool before dipping again. The next time lower candle into the wax dip a few more inches. Remove candle, let wax cool, and repeat this procedure until the whole candle has been dipped. The lower portions of the candle that receive several dippings will have a greater concentration of wax and will consequently be deeper in color than the upper portions.

Color dipping is used extensively by commercial candle companies as the amount of dye needed to color the exterior of a candle is considerably less than for coloring all the way through.

Nothing will weld your decorations to a candle more successfully than a dip in hot wax. However, not all decorations can be dipped. Any protruding surface will cause the wax to drip and this will sometimes spoil the candle.

When using a flower arrangement on the lower portion of a candle, dip candle to just above the decorations. Wipe away any drips on decorations with your finger. There will be drips on the candle but they will be hidden by the flowers. Turn candle over and dip the other half to the line left by first dipping.

Plastic, paper, and cloth flowers benefit greatly from a hot wax dip. If the dipping is carefully done, artificial flowers can often be mistaken for wax flowers. Wax should be quite hot for dipping parchment and cloth flowers so the wax will penetrate instead of merely coating, especially for the first dipping. Some plastics will melt so make a test to be sure wax is not too hot before dipping these.

At least two or three dippings are recommended and each flower must be dipped separately. Never plunge a cluster of flowers into hot wax unless you want a real mess on your hands. When flower is removed from the wax, tap it against the side of container to shake off any excess wax.

Any kind of wax can be used for dipping, but for flowers sculpturing wax works best. Even when cold, it is not brittle and will not crack or break if accidentally dropped or hit.

Antiquing Flowers

Antiquing, or porcelainizing, can turn a Plain Jane plastic flower into a Cinderella, so if you yearn for something to add spice to your flower-bedecked candles, try this:

Mix ½ cup turpentine, ½ cup clear varnish, ¼ teaspoon dark oak stain and ⅛ teaspoon gold powder. Stir mixture well and dip flowers. Shake off excess and hang up to dry.

4

ANY-TIME CANDLES

FEW gifts are appreciated more than an exquisitely decorated candle. Because packaging decorated candles is such a problem, they can't be found in just any store. Trying to locate an elegant candle can be quite a chore and so can locating the money to pay for it. Imagine how nice it will be to make these prized gifts for a dollar or so. A candle of any kind is usually welcome, but a candle keyed to the color scheme and decor of the recipient's home is treasured.

Candles in this chapter are designed for year round accents to add a spice of color. By changing colors from light to dark, they can be used during each of the four seasons. In the spring and summer pastel colors are more appropriate, and in the fall the rich golds, greens, browns, and rusts bring a glow to darker days. Flowers should be used which are in tune with the season.

Dime stores are filled with goodies for decorating your candles and you can lose your mind at a wholesale florist. The florist's stocks are laid in well in advance of a given season and if you want to work on Valentine candles in December, this is where you can find the decorations you need. Stores that sell dress trims have much to offer the candlecrafter. By all means go to a few rummage sales and buy their broken jewelry and flower-trimmed hats. These things usually sell for pennies and that broken earring or millinery flower may be the needed emphasis to complete a charming candle. If you know a window trimmer—one of the people who make those tempting backgrounds for department store windows—consider yourself blessed. They are often delighted to sell their used trimmings for a fraction of original cost. A quick dusting and a couple of dips in hot wax can work wonders on a tired, wilted flower.

Train your eye to look at unlikely objects and see them against the side of a candle. The deeper you delve into candle decorating, the more you will become aware that you are in a field where there are no limits except those you impose yourself.

Flowers and Bases

Flowers are universally loved and this love is carried over into candle decorating. Flower-bedecked candles are everybody's favorites. Probably no other adornment in the candlemaker's bag of tricks can produce such spectacular results with so little time and effort.

A large flower and a leaf or two may be all the embellishment a candle needs or several smaller flowers can be worked into a stunning arrangement. In Illustration No. 15 the candle on left was decorated by pinning on three leaves and inserting a large flower in candle with a hot ice pick. The other candle utilized smaller flowers on stems that were pinned to the candle. Generally, a slightly curved line is more pleasing than a straight row marching up thc side of your candle.

A visit to the local library and a few hours spent studying books on flower arranging can be invaluable in your candle decorating if you would like to know more about design and balance. Many of the books will contain ideas that can be adapted with minor changes to make charming candles.

You will also find much information for combining candles with fresh flowers; not as decoration but as part of an arrangement. Finding the exact color of candle you need for a special arrangement is often impossible, but when you make your own, anything is possible.

For longer lasting arrangements, some of the plastic flowers can successfully compete with nature. Dipping in hot wax eliminates the coldness of plastic and greatly enhances the beauty of the flowers.

Suppose you want to combine flowers and a figurine of some sort. Placing them on the side of a candle is often impractical, but a base would solve everything. Bases for candles may be made of many materials.

Styrofoam is a staple item in the candlecrafter's stock. It can be painted any color and flowers or other decorations glued

Illustration No. 15. Flower-decorated candles.

on or merely pushed into the styrofoam. The old standby circles and squares are in constant demand, but do try the more elaborate stands that dime stores now sell.

Chicken wire, floral netting, upturned bowls, gilded pie tins, plastic doilies, egg cups, coasters, old lamp bases, slabs of wood, and numerous other unrelated items may all be pressed into service when a candle needs a base. One extremely ingenious woman takes her old phonograph records, dips them in boiling water and when they are pliable, turns up four corners. After the records harden, they are sprayed gold and used to hold a candle.

One of the favorite bases is made of wax and becomes a part of the candle. It can be poured when candle is poured in the same or a contrasting color. The need to buy a base is eliminated and your molds are usually on the kitchen shelf. Pie tins, salad molds, bowls, ashtrays, and many other household objects make excellent base molds.

When you pour a candle, pour wax into base mold to a thickness of ½″ to 1″. Bases may be attached with wire or small nails that have almost no heads. If wire is used, cut three pieces about 1″ in length. Wire must be heavy enough so it will not bend easily when pressure is applied to it. With pliers, force half the length of wire pieces into bottom of candle about ¾″ from edge of candle. Position candle over base where it will rest permanently, then press down on candle to push wires through base.

If nails are used, they should be heated before being inserted in wax or holes made for them with a hot icepick. Nails are thicker than the wire and might cause the wax to crack if forced into it.

After base and candle have been fastened together with wire or nails, pour hot wax the color of base into a pie pan and dip base into the hot wax. Wax in the pan should be deep enough to cover the base and about ¼″ of bottom of candle. This will permit the hot wax to flow between base and candle and bond the two together.

In Illustration No. 16 you can see how necessary the base is in making the arrangement with flowers and figurine. Figure may be attached to base with hot wax. Even better adhesion is obtained if figure is dipped along with the base. The same

Illustration No. 16. Candle with wax base.

method will satisfactorily fasten flowers or other ornaments to base.

Tops of palm branches were secured to candle with sequin pins, and flowers were dipped along with base and figurine.

Figure was poured in green and antiqued by rubbing gold, green, and copper bronzing powder over the surface with a finger. For more staying power and a different effect, powder can be sprayed lightly with a clear plastic spray after application to wax. Spraying removes the gloss and leaves a dull or matte finish.

Container Candle with Flowers

A shrimp server can be converted into an out-of-the-ordinary container candle. In Illustration No. 17 the bottom portion, ordinarily filled with ice, was lined with artificial pansies. The bowl section that holds shrimp was poured with purple wax to match the color of the flowers. Gold braid was glued in place on outside of glass. Sequins, glitter, crushed glass, or tiny figurines could be used to decorate the bottom section if desired.

Hand Carved Candles

These candles are fun to make and if you possess artistic ability, you can let yourself go. If drawing is not your forte, back to the idea file you have been collecting. Select a design—a simple one for this project—and transfer it to the candle. This can be done by taping the pattern to candle and with a pin or needle prick holes through the paper to outline design on the wax. The little pin holes in the candle can then be followed as guide lines.

Another method is to hold the pattern against a window, design side toward the pane. Trace design on back of pattern with a china-marking pencil. Tape pattern right side out to candle and with a stylus or ball point pen go over the design, applying moderate pressure. This pressure will transfer the china marking to the wax.

Use these markings for a guide line and gouge out the wax with your carving tools. The indentations can be left as is or painted with hot colored wax or with paints. Glue can be brushed

Illustration No. 17. Crushed-glass decoration and container candle.

in the cavities and glitter sprinkled over the glue. Try dripping sealing wax or melted crayons into these cavities.

Any sharp knife or razor blade can be used for carving, but the job is much easier if inexpensive carving tools from a hobby shop are used. A sturdy, narrow piece of tin that can be bent into a U-shape or V-shape makes an acceptable carving tool. Cover the handle portion with tape to avoid cutting your hand on the raw tin edges.

Carving may be done on a candle of any size, but better results are obtained if candle is large.

Crushed Glass

Crushed glass is equally at home on container or regular candles. All hobby shops carry it and the color selection is vast.

Glue is used for attaching crushed glass to both container and wax candles. Glass is particularly striking on containers as it reflects the light from the candle. Container may be completely covered with glass or it may be used as an accent as in Illustration No. 18.

On the candle in Illustration No. 17, a picture was cut from a magazine and glued to candle. Small gold braid was pinned on candle and crushed glass in blues and greens was glued to candle between the braid and around picture.

Gold cord is useful for outlining a simple design such as a flower, when the flower is to be made of crushed glass.

Stencils

Cut stencils from heavy paper or from regular stencil paper obtainable at an art supply store. Most libraries have books of stencil patterns and detailed instructions for cutting them. Trees, people, flowers, and birds are a few designs that can be incorporated into a stencil. Letters may be cut to spell out "Happy Birthday," "Merry Christmas," or some other greeting.

Tape stencils to candles and paint over the candle surface inside the cut-out area. When painting with hot wax, try to avoid letting the wax come in contact with stencil. If wax should overlap onto a portion of stencil, carefully cut the wax along stencil line before stencil is removed. If this is not done, stencil may

Illustration No. 18. Container candles decorated with crushed glass and jewels.

pull away some of the wax paint that should remain on the candle. This precaution is not necessary when using paints if stencil is removed before paint drys and hardens.

Crushed Eggshells

Instead of tossing your eggshells in the garbage, save them for decorating candles. After white and yolk have been removed, wash the inside of shells and set aside to dry. Place shells between sheets of waxed paper and crush them with a rolling pin. Brush candle with glue and roll candle in the crushed eggshells. A water soluble glue thinned with water brushed over the shell-covered candle will provide additional adhesion.

Large pieces of eggshell can be cut in petal and leaf shapes and fashioned into flowers.

Colored paint or gold or silver sprayed on in either a spatter effect or a solid covering, provides the finishing touch for these candles. Candles may be dipped in hot wax, if desired. When metallic colors are used, dip before colors are applied. Dipping not only dulls the metallics, but will often strip them from the candle.

Lace

This category also includes net, ribbons, and other trimmings. Lacelon ribbon with its light, airy structure is a natural for container or hurricane candles. Unless the candle is quite large, these materials are more appropriate on hurricane or container candles because of the fire hazard. However if candle diameter is of sufficient size so there is no danger of decorations coming in contact with candle flame, use them anywhere.

Decorations can be sewn to net and net then wrapped around candle and glued or sewn in place. Net ruffles provide a feminine touch for a young girl's bedroom.

Try covering a tall, straight container with heavy lace. Glue lace in place and when glue has dried, brush several coats of clear varnish or shellac over the lace. Lace may then be highlighted with touches of color, or for something really unusual, brush on the antiquing mixture made for porcelainizing or antiquing plastic flowers.

Candle in Illustration No. 19 was poured in dark blue and trimmed with heavy white lace. More contrast is provided if dark colors are used with white lace. Lace was dipped in clear sculpturing wax several times and wax was removed from any clogged holes in the lace. Lace was fastened to candle with hot wax.

Paper

Painting a detailed scene on a candle is a difficult task that requires patience and talent. Patience is something all candlecrafters acquire, but talent is harder to come by. The less artistically inclined can have beautifully painted candles by using rice paper.

Rice paper has the happy faculty of becoming transparent when wet. This means you can paint a design on rice paper, wrap it around a candle, dip in hot wax, and the painting appears to be on the candle and not the paper. It is also thin enough so tracing can be done with ease. Find a design you like, transfer it to rice paper, and paint.

Most paints seem to work well on this paper, even a set of dime store water colors. To be on the safe side, though, before you invest your time in a complicated painting, make a few brush strokes on a small piece of rice paper. When paint is dry, dip paper in hot wax and see how the paint reacts.

Cut paper to fit candle before you begin your painting. Paper can cover candle completely or the design only can be applied to candle. Liquid glue will stick paper to wax but even better is the dry-stick glue used by photographers. It is packaged in a spray can, will not wet paper and dries almost immediately. Try a photographic shop for this item.

After painted paper has been glued to candle, dip in hot wax and presto—a beautifully painted candle.

Wet tissue paper has a transparent quality that can be useful for decoration. Tear small strips of different colored tissue and glue them to candle. Strips can be put on in a random pattern or in rows of color. An example could be pink tissue strips near the bottom of candle and the second row yellow with some of the yellow overlapping the pink. Finish off at the top with blue and let some of it overlap the yellow. When candle is

Illustration No. 19. Candles decorated with lace and brocade tools.

dipped, your colors will include pink, orange, yellow, green, and blue.

Madras tissue, with its subtle blending of colors, is lovely on candles.

Fire Resistance

It seems a good idea to make this the next item after paper. A large number of candle decorations will burn if they come in contact with a flame. To reduce this hazard, flameproof your more flammable materials with sodium silicate. The common name for this product is "water glass" and it can be found in any drugstore. Paper and plastic flowers can be dipped in this substance before being waxed. For the tissue and rice paper candles, brush on a coating of water glass and let dry before dipping. If these precautions are followed, only charring will result from contact with candle flame.

Brocade Tools

These are little wire tools with wooden handles. The wire ends are bent into various shapes and by dipping the tools into paint, the outline of the wire can be transferred to another surface. Brocade tools were designed for the ceramics trade and are available in ceramic shops.

A high-pile design is possible if thick paint is used and several applications made on top of each other.

Tape was used on the glass container in Illustration No. 19 so painted strips would be straight and clean. Large flowers were made with the No. 8 tool and the small ones with the No. 9 tool. Brocade tool was dipped into paint and then pressed against the glass. Dots were made by dipping the point of a tool in paint and transfering to glass.

The points on candle in Illustration No. 19 were outlined with tape before painting. Decoration is a combination of painting and tools. Background area was given a solid coat of paint and tape removed. Scalloped border was formed with Tool No. 11. Some of the flowers were painted on and some were made with brocade tools.

Detailed directions for use are included with each set of

tools and a variety of designs and accents can be applied to candles with swiftness and ease.

Wax Cutouts

This one calls for simple design. Pour a thin sheet of sculpturing wax. Sheet can be flattened with a rolling pin if it is poured too thick. Fold sheet around candle and cut to exact size. Using paper cutouts for patterns, cut design in the wax sheet. Wrap sheet around candle and seal with hot wax. Color of wax sheet should not be the same as candle as the contrast where candle is visible through cutouts is necessary for this candle to be effective.

Pieces that were cut from wax sheet may be saved and applied to another candle for silhouette decoration.

Doilies

Interesting and sometimes slightly weird designs can be transferred to candles by using paper doilies. Tape doily to candle and spray paint. The cut-out designs in the doily will be the painted areas on the candle.

Filigree Hurricane

Candles like these are rarely seen in candle shops as they are so uncommon that few people are familiar with them.

Pour a hurricane candle as usual and while wax shell is still in mold and before it hardens, cut around one of the sides with a knife or razor blade. When shell is removed from mold, gently push this side out of candle.

Cut a paper pattern for a new front for your hurricane. It won't matter if the sides extend beyond the wax shell. In fact, this will give you more scope for an unusual border. Pour wax into a pan about the same thickness as the three remaining sides of the shell. Lay pattern over wax when it becomes firm and cut a new front for the candle.

The main thing to avoid is having too much open area. The idea for the cut-outs in Illustration No. 20 was borrowed from a picture of a snowflake. Other designs could be polka dots, moon and stars, leaves, abstracts, lightning bolts, tear drops, and many others.

When front is hard attach to shell with hot wax or by quickly running a wood-burning tool or small soldering iron along the seam where the pieces fit together.

Travertine Candles

Would you like to know how to make a travertine candle? So would the rest of us candlecrafters. This is one candlemaking secret that hasn't been sleuthed out yet. It may be common knowledge tomorrow, but right now we are all still guessing.

Travertines are candles with a gold leaf imbedded in them and the leaf seems to disappear into the interior of the candle. Usually these candles are white but are occasionally poured in light pastels.

Although I can't give you instructions for a genuine travertine, there are some acceptable substitutes.

Special foils are sold in candle supply houses that give a good imitation of this type candle. The foils are crumpled and inserted in mold and candle is then poured

The application of pieces of gold leaf produces a prettier candle than the use of crumpled foil. After candle has been taken from mold, spray glue on candle and apply pieces of gold leaf. Gold leaf must be handled with tender, loving care. You almost have to hold your breath while working with it as a medium sized sigh can shatter one of the fragile sheets. Once leaf is securely attached, carefully dip candle in hot wax. Results are better if pieces applied to candle are not uniform in size.

Ball Candles

For a long time it was necessary to use a round bowl if you had a yen for a ball candle. There just weren't any round molds. Finally, ball molds were made of plastic and, frankly, they were very little improvement over the bowls. Now it is possible to buy metal ball molds that are easy to use and make lovely ball candles. The sizes available are still limited. Most beginners prefer to invest in the conventional candle molds and the ball candles discussed here will be made by the bowl technique.

Pour wax into bowl and after hardened wax is removed,

pour again to make the other half of the ball. Before wax hardens, insert ice pick in center for wick hole. After both halves are removed, check holes to be sure they extend all the way through the wax. Thread wick through the lower half of ball.

Sections may be joined by using whipped wax or by pouring a thin sheet of sculpturing wax the color of ball and placing it on bottom half as soon as it is firm enough to be moved. Thread wick through top section and press the two halves together. Trim off any excess wax that seeps out between the sections.

The major drawback to these candles is that the joining line is so apparent. Ball can be dipped in hot wax to aid in concealing this line or ball can be textured as was done on this candle. (Illustration No. 20.)

Dogwood blossoms and leaves were poured in a mold with sculpturing wax. Tree limbs were rolled from brown sculpturing wax and fastened with hot wax to candle. Blossoms and leaves were placed over the top of candle and around the branches. Centers and edges of flowers were touched with gold.

Illustration No. 20. Ball candle with dogwood and filigree hurricane.

Finger Painting

Finger painting can be just a few sweeps and squiggles or a real painting. Sweeps and squiggles are about the extent of my finger painting abilities as is very evident in Illustration No. 21.

If you can't stand being a mess up to your elbows, forget finger painting. The best way to get the paint on the candle is to cover your palms with it and then wipe them on the candle. Designs can be made with your fingers, nails, heel and sides of hands. About the only instructions that can be given are to start making marks on the candle until you do something you like and then keep going. If paint dries before this happens, spread on another coat and continue.

Polymer plastic paints, which have been thinned considerably with polymer varnish, perform quite well as a painting medium on wax. When painting is completed and dry, a dip in hot wax will make it permanent.

Swirl Candles

A container taller than candle and an inch or two wider is a must for these candles. Fill container with lukewarm water and put drops of paint on top of the water. This must be done carefully. If paint is poured into water, it is likely to sink to the bottom of container and for this candle to be successful, paint must stay on the surface. Put paint in a spoon and with the back of spoon touching the water, slowly roll it so paint slides out. One or more colors may be used.

When paint has been deposited on water, very gently stir the water—not the paint—so water commences a slow circular motion. Holding candle by wick, lower it into the paint-covered water. Push paint to one side when withdrawing candle so it will not receive a second coat on the way up.

Sea Shells

Sea shells are striking on either container or molded candles. Sea fern, sea fans, sea horses, small starfish, aquarium pebble and shells, large and small, are all appropriate for decoration. (Illutration No. 21.)

5

SPECIAL OCCASION CANDLES

A CANDLE for a wedding, shower, or anniversary is rarely easy to find. The ones you do find in the stores usually consist of a covering of whipped wax embellished with a tired looking spray of lily of the valley.

Speciality candles of this type are no harder to make than any other and I have always wondered why there were so few attractive one available.

Wedding

Let's start with wedding candles. At one time only white was considered appropriate for a wedding candle, but pastel colors are gaining in popularity, particularly for second weddings. All of the candles shown here were done in color because of the difficulty in getting sharp photographic detail from an all-white candle.

Lily of the valley, roses, orchids, and orange blossoms seem to be the favorite for wedding candles, although any flower may be used. If the candle is for a large wedding, check with the florist to find out what flowers will be used at the church and reception. Key your candle decorations accordingly. Some brides will have quite definite ideas of the type of candle wanted and others will be vague and leave it up to you.

If you plan to sell candles, particularly wedding candles, it would be good business to take pictures of your wedding candles as they are made. Use these pictures to build a wedding candle book that prospective brides could look through. The photographs will show what you are capable of and will also help the customer decide on exactly the candle she wants.

Orange blossom scent is the favorite for a wedding candle, but if it is to be custom made rather than a stock candle, check to see what the bride's preference is.

Net, lace, and pearls are appropriate trimmings for wedding candles. Small bibles, either real or made of wax, dime store engagement and wedding ring sets, and crosses fit into the wedding decor.

Praying Hands

Wedding ceremonies are usually moving, religious occasions and this can be carried out in the candle. In our modern world marriage counsellors, psychiatrists, family doctors, and ministers are often needed to hold some marriages together so something that suggests a prayer for the newlyweds would not be out of line.

These hands are from a plaster mold and the detail is so exquisite that it seems a waste to lose this detail by dipping. Excess wax on bottom of hands left from the pouring spout should not be cut off. The protruding wax will serve as an anchor when placing the hands in whipped wax. If it is not left in place, the cuffs must be pushed into the wax and partially covered. Place hands in the whipped wax while it is still warm and sprinkle on glitter.

Bells were also made from a mold but other kinds of bells could be substituted. Filigree plastic bells stocked by candle supply and cake decorating houses are attractive on wedding candles and come in several sizes. Bells can also be made by using small wine glasses for molds. Pour wax in glass, let a thin shell form and pour out the liquid wax.

An acceptable clapper may be fashioned by threading wire through a bead, bending end of wire to prevent head slipping off and dipping wire and bead in hot wax. Place the other end of the wire inside the bell. Turn bell upside down, prop in place and pour in a small amount of hot wax to hold wire in place.

Thin strips of sculpturing wax were used for the ribbon. Two long strips were cut for the ends of bow and fastened to candle first. Bow was made by looping the ends of short strips together and attaching to candle with hot wax. Bells were placed

Illustration No. 26. Bride and Groom, rings and orchids, and praying hands.

in the center of bow and small flowers filled in any bare spots. (Illustration No. 26.)

Wedding Tapers

Lily of the valley sprays were dipped in hot wax and bent slightly so that an arch was formed when they were placed on candle. The small plastic bride and groom were dipped in hot wax before they were attached to candle beneath the arch. Three small flowers applied with hot wax beneath each figure complete the candle. (Illustration No. 27.)

Candles such as these can be made in less than ten minutes. Even buying the tapers retail, a handsome profit can be realized by selling these wedding tapers for $2.50 or $3.00.

Rings

The giant rings are really plastic bracelets from the dime store. Rings were sprayed gold before the jewels were put on. Floral adhesive, which is excellent for attaching lightweight dec-

Illustration No. 27. Wedding tapers and bells and ribbons.

orations to candles, holds the diamonds in place on the rings. A large stone from an old pin was used for the engagement rings and a mounting of floral adhesive was built up around the bracelet to hold the stone. When stone was in place, mounting was trimmed and then painted gold to match the rest of the ring. Small dots of adhesive placed on the back of the small rhinestones fastened them to the rings.

Slip rings over top of candle and attach to candle with hot wax. The small flowers between rings act as separators as well as decoration.

Four plastic orchids were pinned near the bottom of candle and a net ruffle twined between flowers, covering stems and pin heads. (Illustration No. 26.)

Ribbons and Bells

The next time you need ideas for wedding candles, go to a card shop and browse. Many of the designs on wedding cards can be adapted for candles—in fact, that's where this idea came from.

Five large wax bells were attached to front of candle. Long, narrow strips of sculpturing wax cut from a sheet were looped around and between bells while the wax was still warm and pliable. Where ribbon touched candle or bells it was secured with hot wax. Flowers and some splashes of gold paint were added for the finishing touch. (Illustration No. 27.)

Bride and Groom

The cake decorating supply houses are probably your best single source of decorations for wedding candles. Many of the items they sell for wedding cake ornaments are excellent for candles. Wedding candles can not only be keyed to the wedding flowers, but also follow the same decorating scheme as used on the wedding cake.

For this candle a mound of whipped wax was placed slightly above the middle of candle. Three filagree bells were pushed into the whipped wax. Above the bells two large flowers were also inserted in the wax. Smaller flowers were glued to candle under the bells. Candle was attached to base and the base covered with whipped wax. While wax was still warm, a plastic bride and groom was inserted in the wax. Flowers were pushed into the whipped wax around the edge of the base. (Illustration No. 26.)

Shower Candles

Wedding candles can often do double duty as wedding, shower, or engagement party candles. If the colors are appropriate, a flower decorated candle with no special theme may be used for a wedding or a shower.

Umbrellas

Umbrellas are almost traditional for showers and can cover almost any kind of shower. Here is a candle that, with minor changes in decoration, can be used for various kinds of showers.

From the party favor counter of the dime store get some small plastic umbrellas and dip them in hot wax. Cut out a small hole in the side of candle. Place edge of umbrella in this hole and fasten with hot wax. Attach umbrella handle to candle with hot wax. Glue small flowers on umbrella and scatter flowers around bottom of candle. (Illustration No. 28.)

This candle can be varied by turning umbrellas upside down. Fill umbrellas with flowers, using glue to keep them in place. Fasten umbrellas to candle in same manner as candle illustrated.

To indicate that such a candle is for a baby shower, place small wax or plastic baby figures on candle so it appears that they are sitting on umbrella handles and flowers. (Illustration No. 28.)

Instead of flowers, umbrellas could be filled with small packages, doll-sized kitchen utensils, pieces of material folded to represent linens, etc.

One of my most popular umbrella shower candles was made with a cone mold. A hole about 1½″ deep was cut in center of bottom of candle and a short wooden dowel inserted in hole. Candle was placed upside down in a heavy glass and dowel propped so it was absolutely straight. Hole was then filled with very hot wax. Candle should not be touched until wax in hole is cold and hard.

When wax has hardened and candle could be moved, six pieces of small cord were pinned lengthwise around candle to represent the umbrella ribs. A small amount of whipped wax

Illustration No. 28. Umbrella shower candles.

was placed on top of candle and molded to a point around the wick. Small flowers were then placed in the whipped wax.

A net ruffle was pinned around the bottom of candle so it formed a scallop with the point at each of the gold ribs. Gold cord was pinned over the net to cover raw edges. Flower was placed at the point of each scallop.

A deep base was poured in a fluted salad mold and a hole cut in the center of the base. The other end of the dowel was inserted in this hole, candle propped straight, and hole filled with hot wax. Base can be left plain or scattered with flowers.

Package Candle

Carve small squares and rectangles of wax and convert them into packages with bows, ribbons, and tiny flowers. Using a bootie mold, pour booties and insert a wick in each one by punching a hole with a hot icepick. Decorate front of booties with ribbons or flowers. Pin or glue a ribbon to each of the booties and fasten the other end of the ribbon to candle. Place a package over the end of ribbon and fasten it with hot wax. Scatter the other packages over the candle. (Illustration No. 29.)

Baby Shower

Wax decorations were used for this candle but baby items from the toy counter of the dime store can be substituted. All the decorations on the candle, as well as booties, are available in one mold. Wax castings can be attached to candle with hot wax, small wire, or straight pins with the heads clipped off. (Illustration No. 29.)

A great number of baby shower candles can be made using a diaper motif. Cut small triangles of sculpturing wax, fold to form a diaper, and fasten with a small gold pin or tiny flower. Fasten several of these diapers to candle with hot wax.

Or you might twine a length of gold cord around a candle to represent a clothesline. Attach the small diapers to the clothesline with hot wax.

Cut a large triangle of sculpturing wax and cut a hole in the center large enough to fit over a candle. Slide the triangle over the candle and then fasten the three corners with a large safety pin. Attach the top edges of diaper to candle with hot wax.

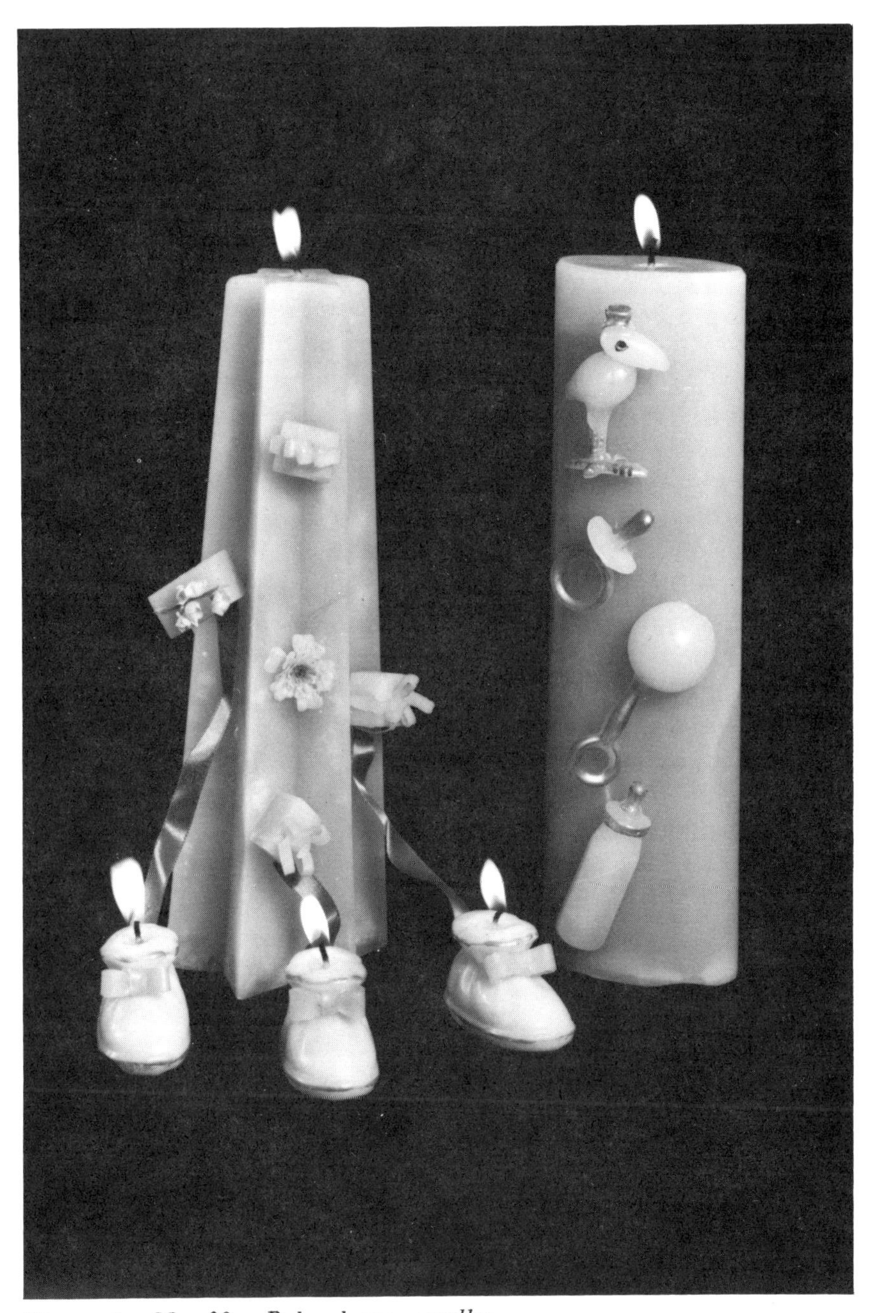

Illustration No. 29. Baby shower candles.

Announcement

A wedding candle can be converted to a candle for the announcement party by adding the wedding date.

Here's an idea for a centerpiece for an announcement that can be as simple or as elaborate as you care to make it. Either use styrofoam or pour a large rectangular base of wax. Place a candle at each end of the rectangle and attach to the candles a ribbon swag lettered with the names of the bride and groom and the date of the wedding. The lettering can be done with glitter glue in a tube. Add a few flowers on the base and you have your simple centerpiece. For a more elaborate one, place a small bride and groom between the candles, add bells, flowers, ribbons, etc.

Not everyone thinks the young lovers shown in Illustration No. 30 are as appealing as I do, so be sure the recipient would prefer this to the hearts and flowers. Usually, the younger the bride, the better she likes a candle of this type.

After couple has been poured and painted, attach them to the base with a small amount of floral adhesive. It might also be added protection to attach them to the candle with wire and hot wax. Add the flowers to the base and dip the base and decorations. Flowers may be pinned on the sides of candle.

Another use for this couple is with a tree stump mold. Carve initials of the engaged couple on the stump and surround with a carved heart. The base may be covered with flowers, hearts, or even some tiny animals.

This couple is equally at home on a Valentine candle.

Anniversary

The biggest demand for anniversary candles is for Silver or Golden Wedding Anniversaries, but there is no reason why all anniversaries shouldn't be celebrated with an appropriate candle.

The various anniversaries are: 1—paper; 2—cotton; 3—leather; 4—fruit, flowers, or books; 5—wooden; 6—candy; 7—woolen: 8—pottery or bronze; 9—willow or straw; 10—tin; 12—silk and linen; 15—crystal; 20—china; 25—silver; 30—pearl; 40—ruby or emerald; 50—golden; 60–70–75—diamond.

Illustration No. 30. Announcement.

Here are some ideas that could be used for decorating various anniversary candles:

Paper—pennants cut from plain paper or from metallic foil. On these pennants names, dates, or Happy Anniversary can be written with felt markers, gold paint, or glue and glitter. Roll pennants around toothpicks and place in a row around bottom of candle or glue on sides. Small paper fans, paper parasols, foil medallions, or paper cut-outs could also be used.

Cotton—bolls of real cotton or cotton-ball fringe.

Leather—cut designs from an old leather purse or use pieces of a hand tooled leather belt.

Fruit, flowers or books—plastic fruit or flowers, bookmarks or small pieces of paper cut and folded to resemble books. Label the books with titles appropriate to the history of the marriage.

Wooden—popsickle sticks, wooden upholstery pins, wooden beads.

Candy—hard candy glued to candle or jelly beans or gum drops stuck on with pins.

Pottery or bronze—bronze or pottery figurines, bronze coins or candle sprayed with bronze paint.

Willow or straw—small raffia baskets or cornucopias.

Tin—cut pieces of tin can into shapes and apply to candle by punching holes in tin and pinning.

Silk and linen—cover container candle with a thin piece of printed silk.

Crystal—toy glasses.

Silver—silver candle, silver medallions, silver painted flowers or figures.

Pearl—old jewelry.

Ruby or emerald—red or green candle and old jewelry.

Gold—see examples in this chapter.

Diamond—rhinestones and large glass jewelry.

Anniversary Cherubs

Two wax cherubs painted gold were attached to sides of candle with small wires and hot wax. Chrysanthemum leaves were pinned in place and large white chrysanthemum was put on with a hot icepick. The candle and decorations were sprayed lightly with gold paint and when paint was dry, shield was pinned in place. (Illustration No. 31.)

Illustration No. 31. Anniversary candles.

Anniversary shields are available in silver and gold for 25th and 50th anniversaries.

Anniversary Heart

A plastic lattice heart designed to be used on a wedding cake was filled with flowers by winding the flower stems in and out of the lattice work. Flowers and heart were secured to candle with hot wax and pins. Decorations and candle were sprayed with gold and anniversary shield then pinned in place. (Illustration No. 31.)

Either of the above candles can be converted to a Silver Wedding Anniversary candle by sibstituting silver paint for the gold and using a 25th anniversary shield.

Birthday

Anything that would appeal to a child is suitable for a small fry's birthday candle. It can be something universally appealing, such as a circus, or something more personalized to tie in with a particular child's interest. The cake decorating houses have birthday decorations ranging from the cave man to the space age.

Illustration No. 32. Birthday candles.

Clown

The clown candle is not hard to make and is loved by the younger set. A cone mold is used for this candle. Half of it can be poured in one color—for the hat—and another color for the face, or a single color may be used for the entire candle as was done in Illustration No. 32. Hat portion of candle can be painted for contrast or stripes, polka dots, or other designs might be painted on.

Ruffles are made by cutting thin strips of sculpturing wax and fluting the strips with your fingers. Strips can be applied to candle with hot wax or a small soldering iron. When joining two ruffled strips together, dip the end of one strip in hot wax and quickly press it against the end of the other strip.

The ruff around the clown's neck consists of three rows of ruffles. One row of ruffles is placed around the bottom of hat near the middle of candle. Whip some wax and put a ball of it around the wick at top of candle. Paint on a happy face to smile at the youngsters.

If you want to continue the circus motif, make a cage of wild animals. Pour a candle without a wick in a square hurricane mold. Pour the animals in plastic animal half molds and fasten animals to sides of candle. This candle will be long rather than tall, so place it on one side before putting on the animals. About ⅓ of the distance from each end of top of candle, punch two holes with a hot icepick and insert wick in each hole.

Roll tiny strips of sculpturing wax and place them vertically around the cage to represent bars. Cut a scalloped border out of wax and place it around the top of cage. Cut a straight strip for the border around bottom of cage.

Carve two rectangles of wax the width of cage and place under candle. Either pour or cut four round wax discs for the wheels. Wheels and the two rectangles should be positioned so they are in line. The rectangles are to hold the candle off the table so no weight will be on the wheels. The wheels are for show and not for holding up the cage. Attach the wheels to the rectangles with wire and hot wax and then fasten rectangles to bottom of cage.

Paint spokes on the wheels, features on the animals and the name of the child on the cage. If the candle says "Bobby's Circus Wagon" it becomes much more treasured than if it were just any circus wagon.

Nursery Rhymes

Nursery rhymes never grow old and pictures illustrating these jingles are always in favor with children. Candlecrafters like them too because of the speed with which they can be put together.

Cut pictures from an old book or birthday wrapping paper and paste on candle. Some of the shorter rhymes could also be pasted on if a child has a particular favorite. Either dip candle in hot wax or brush hot wax over the pictures. A sprinkling of glass beads will provide added charm. (Illustration No. 32.)

Toy Soldiers

A single sentry or a parade is possible with this candle. Pour a small round candle in white and cover the top 2″ with whipped wax. This whipped wax becomes the hat and it can be applied in color or painted later. Paint a face under the hat and criss-cross two strips of plastic tape across his chest. Circle the candle with a piece of tape approximately where his chin would be and put another piece of tape around candle for a belt. The two circles of tape should cover the ends of the crossed pieces of tape. To go a step farther, arms could be cut from sculpturing wax and placed stiffly at his sides or smartly saluting.

Castle

How about an ancient castle? Two candles will be needed for this one—a hurricane and a round candle. Hurricane mold may be poured as a hurricane or as a solid candle.

Cut off a corner of the square candle and seal the tall round candle into the hole with hot wax. Build up a cone shape on the top of the round candle with whipped wax. Cut a circle of sculpturing wax and slit circle to the center. Lap the edges over until a cone is formed that will fit over the top of the round candle. Trim off overlapping ends and seal with hot wax. The parapet on the square candle is made by cutting square grooves in a strip of sculpturing wax and sealing this strip to top of candle.

With a knife or woodburning tool, cut or burn grooves in both candles to represent stones, leaving a solid space for door and window. Paint door and windows. (Illustration No. 32.)

For the very ambitious, a heavy sheet of wax might be poured for a drawbridge. Chain from an old necklace could be attached to candle and end of bridge to represent chain to raise and lower bridge. Some plastic knights engaged in a tournament or even a fire-breathing dragon could make this a very exciting centerpiece.

Decals

All the candle supply houses have birthday decals. These are marked off by years—some of them up to 21. Candles are saved from year to year and on the birthday they are burned down to the next number.

Graduation

A party for the graduate certainly calls for a candle to celebrate the occasion.

A diploma can be fashioned from a small rolled sheet of paper tied with a ribbon and used for decoration. A passable facsimile of a diploma is a round white candle tied in the middle with a ribbon. Cake decorating houses have numerous plastic figures to tie in with a graduation theme.

Mortar Board

Pour a candle in a large bowl and before wax hardens make a hole in the middle for wick. Pour a sheet of wax in a square pan. When square is cold, remove and place on top of candle. cutting a hole in the middle for wick. Roll some sculpturing wax fairly thin and attach it to top of candle and either mold fringe from wax or use cloth fringe and fasten it to other end of roll and to side of square. (Illustration No. 33.)

Illustration No. 33. Graduation Cap.

6

HOLIDAY CANDLES

MAYBE it's because holidays are special days, but whatever the reason, it's more fun to make holiday candles than any other kind. Valentine's Day, Easter, and Christmas are the favorite times for candlecraftsmen, with Christmas leading the field.

Holiday candles seem to be easier to make than others, maybe because decorations used for these candles leave no doubt as to their purpose. Making exactly the right candle to fit into the living room decor involves decisions—but a Santa Claus-decorated candle is always right for the Christmas season.

New Years

Since this is the first holiday of the year, we'll start out with a candle for the occasion. If you have a New Year's party, by all means have a New Year's candle at the party. Perhaps we should all put a light—candle light, of course—in the window to guide the return of the brave resolutions that slipped away into the darkness soon after they were made.

All other holidays really begin when we get out of bed on the holiday morning, but the New Year begins on the stroke of midnight. So—put a clock on your candle. An ambitious project would be a grandfather clock made from strips of sculpturing wax. For something not so complicated, outline the face of a clock with sequins, nailheads or soft wax. Pieces of plastic tape can be cut quickly to fashion hands pointing to 12. The numerals might be suggested by sequins, rhinestones, colored pinheads, or the numbers painted on.

Paper hats used as part of the New Year's celebration are

too large to put on a candle, but they can be copied in wax in smaller versions. Make a cone for the crown by cutting a circle of sculpturing wax and slitting circle to center. Overlap the cut ends until cone is the size wanted, trim off the overlap, and seal with hot wax. A circle of wax with a hole in the center will serve as a brim. Several of these hats in gay colors would be quite festive on a white candle.

Spray a candle with glitter cement and sprinkle it with confetti. Cut long thin strips of soft wax and curl them around your finger. Straighten the strips out slightly and drape them over and around the candle to give the impression of tossed paper streamers.

Masks are another traditional New Year's decoration and they can be easily made from sculpturing wax. Cut an oval from a sheet of wax and cut two holes for the eyes in the oval. With a pencil or some other small round object bend out some of the wax below the eye holes for a nose. These masks can be left unadorned or spruced up with glitter, sequins, or lace trim.

Valentine's Day

Hearts, flowers, and romance. What a ball candlecrafters have with these candles.

Remember the candy hearts with "I love you" and "Be Mine" lettered on them? They are still sold at the dime stores and a bagfull can enliven a number of candles. Put them on a candle with glue or floral adhesive.

In fact, anything goes as far as hearts are concerned. Make them out of wax, sequins, silver or gold foil, glue and glitter, or cut them from old Valentines. Pour a base for your candle in a heart-shaped cake pan and trim it with net ruffles.

Don't forget decals when you decorate for Valentine, especially if you need something in a hurry. You'll find decals in flower swags, birds, butterflies, cherubs, hearts and arrows, and all of them can make quick work of a Valentine candle. Candle in Illustration No. 34 is decorated entirely with decals.

The tapers in Illustration No. 34 combine hearts, flowers, ruffles, and cherubs to leave no doubt that these candles are for Valentine's Day. The ruffle was pinned to the candle and the

Illustration No. 34. Valentine candles.

heart placed over the ruffle and attached with hot wax. The two roses and cherubs were also fastened to candle with hot wax.

The idea for this candle can be adapted for a larger candle by using larger hearts and flowers. Hearts can be cut from a sheet of sculpturing wax, and made as large or small as needed. The cherubs are from a plaster mold.

Easter

Ask any candlecrafter the day after Valentine's Day what he is doing and the reply usually is "working on my Easter candles." Easter seems to inspire more candlemakers than any other holiday except Christmas.

Egg Candles

Long before Easter begin saving all your eggshells. Anytime you need an egg other than for frying, take a little extra time to get the egg out. Punch a small hole in the little end of the egg with an icepick. At the other end peel off the shell until you have a hole about the size of your fingernail. Remove the egg by blowing through the small hole. Rinse the inside of shells

Illustration No. 35. Easter candles.

with a mixture of vinegar and water and put them aside to dry.

Before using the shells for candles, pour a little cooking oil inside, plug the holes with your fingers and shake to coat the inside of shell with oil. Drain the oil from each shell and insert a wick. Put a piece of clay or tape over the hole and wick in small end of egg. Save the cardboard cartons the eggs are sold in and put the shells in them to hold mold upright during pouring. Pour colored wax into shells, refilling if necessary.

When wax is hard, peel shells from wax. It will probably be necessary to dip the candles in hot wax to smooth the surface. Decorate these little eggs with glitter, tiny flowers, sequins, gold or silver foil, melted crayons, paint, bits of jewelry, or sealing wax. Smooth and level the bottom of candle so it will stand without tipping over.

Hide a few of these candles with the Easter eggs and when the hunt is over, light them while the eggs are being eaten. The children will love it.

Easter Egg Tree

About 30 eggs are required to cover this tree. A large hole can be made in the side of egg shell for removing egg, as only half the shell will be used for a mold. Rinse and oil the inside of shells and then pour in different colors. Don't fill the shell completely, only about half full as you don't want a full round egg for this one. Pour candle in a cone mold and begin your decorating at the top. Eggs should extend slightly above the top of candle so they form a point. Eggs may be attached to candle individually with hot wax or an area covered with whipped wax and the eggs quickly pressed into it. Place eggs as close together as you can in order to minimize the bare area. It will be impossible to solidly cover the candle with eggs, but the gaps between them can be filled in with small flowers or bits of jewelry. Eggs may be decorated before or after they are placed on the candle.

Your candle will have a more pleasing appearance if all your eggs are pretty much the same size. The small, medium, or large eggs may be used but they should not be mixed.

Eggs and Bunnies

In Illustration No. 35 the eggs are hollow and filled with flowers and other decorations. These hollow eggs are made by pouring wax into a fairly large hole made in the side of the shell and removing liquid wax after a thin shell forms. Peel off the shell and trim the windows or openings.

Glue decorations inside the wax shells and then decorate the outside. Wax shells were placed in the niches of a pointed star candle and fastened with hot wax. Rabbits were painted and placed above the eggs. A base of Easter grass is optional.

Panorama Easter Egg

When I was small I thought the sugar panorama eggs with Easter scenes inside were the most fascinating things in the world. These can be created in wax and although they can't be called candles, they are impressive and ornamental conversation pieces.

The candle supply houses all have large egg molds or the dime stores at Easter usually have hollow plastic eggs in all sizes. Most of these have two pieces that fit together like a box, and they can be converted to candle molds quite easily by drilling a small hole at the top for the wick and a larger hole at the bottom for pouring. Fasten them tightly together with rubber bands and seal the sides with tape or clay to prevent wax leakage. These are general instructions for pouring a solid egg candle.

With the panorama egg, do not put the two halves together, but pour them separately. When shell is of sufficient thickness, pour out the center wax. Build up a scene of some sort in the bottom half of shell. Chenille chicks, bunnies, nests of tiny hand molded wax eggs, Easter lilies, cross, or small Madonna are some of the decorations that might be used. Occasionally hold the top half of the egg over the bottom half to be certain the decorations will not be so tall as to prevent the two halves fitting together properly.

When all decorations are in place, fit the two halves together and seal with hot wax. Cut a window in the front of the egg for viewing and put flowers, ribbons, sequins, or other ornaments on top and sides of egg and around window.

These eggs will be picked up and peeped into many times so be extra careful that all decorations are put on to stay.

Window Candle

Candle on left in Illustration No. 35 was also poured in a large plastic egg mold with each half being poured separately.

However, with this egg one half is solid and the other half a shell. While the shell is still in the mold and before it has completely hardened, cut a large hole in the center. When shell is removed from mold it will be easy to pop out the cut portion of the wax. Place a wick across the center of the solid half of the egg and hold it in place by brushing with hot wax. Seal the two halves together with hot wax. You now have an egg that is half solid wax and half shell. Through the opening cut in the center of shell pour in hot wax the same or contrasting color until the shell is filled to within about 1″ of the opening. Let wax harden and then insert your decorations inside the shell.

Another method would be to carefully spoon whipped wax into the opening in the shell and before it hardens place your decorations in it.

Pearl strips, sequins, or glitter can be used to cover seam line made by joining the two halves. Don't put too much decoration on the outside of candle or it will draw attention from the decoration inside.

Easter Bonnet

My hat wardrobe consists of a white hat for weddings and a black hat for funerals. When other people are shopping for new Easter bonnets to cover their heads, I'm usually making one to brighten my table.

A round plastic refrigerator bowl can perform double duty as a mold for the hat crown. Wick can be inserted by the hot ice pick method after wax is removed or hole can be made in the wax while it is still in mold but before it has hardened.

Cut a circular brim from a large sheet of wax and place the crown in the center of the circle. Fasten the two together with hot wax or whipped wax. A very feminine hat can be made by crumpling a folded strip of net and fastening it to the brim. Wind ribbon around the bottom of the crown to cover raw edges. Edges may also be hidden with a row of flowers.

A more tailored hat, such as a sailor, should have a shallower crown, so don't fill the mold all the way. Join crown and brim and circle bottom of crown with a length of grosgrain ribbon. A couple of daisies in front of the ribbon and you will have an Easter hat to burn.

Easter Basket

An Easter basket candle is very appropriate for Easter and children love it. The basket shown in Illustration No. 35 is made of wax from a plaster mold, but a wire basket could be used. Metal baskets are a frequent favorite for flower arrangements and are not hard to find. If a metal basket is used, line it with aluminum foil to keep the liquid wax from leaking out.

The basket mold used for this candle has a handle, but it is doubtful that it could withstand the direct heat from the candle flame. Make another handle by curving a long piece of wire and wrapping a strip of wax around it. Wax covering for the wire should be the same color as the basket. Be sure to keep the handle high so the heat will be dissipated somewhat by the time it reaches the handle.

Green whipped wax can be used to simulate grass and also for anchoring the decorations. The wax may be left soft and fluffy or scratched with the tines of a fork.

This Easter basket utilized flowers, eggs, and bunnies. Flowers may be made by hand or poured in a mold. Wax rabbits from a mold were used in this case, but chenille or plastic ones from the dime store would substitute beautifully. If chenille or plastic rabbits are used, keep them near the edge of the basket and away from the flame. The "eggs" are small jelly beans that have been dipped in wax. These jelly beans make very acceptable little eggs when they are coated in wax. Just stick a toothpick in one side and dip the jelly bean in hot wax two or three times.

Dig two holes in the top of basket near the sides and insert the handle. Fasten it with hot wax. Cover the top of the basket with green whipped wax, being particularly careful to cover the section where the handle and basket join. Mound the whipped wax in the center of basket and insert your decorations in the wax while it is still warm. A final touch might be a small bow on the handle.

The first impulse when seeing this candle is to pick it up by the handle to examine it. This can be disastrous so watch it carefully or attach a small sign on the handle to discourage this.

If you don't have a basket mold, make do with a fluted jello mold. The addition of a handle and some whipped wax grass will make a very convincing basket. You will also find that you have a larger decorating area and can use wax eggs made from empty egg shells as all or part of the decoration. Make and attach a handle in the same manner as was done with the molded basket.

Taper Calla Lily

A large, economy size calla lily can be made in a matter of minutes with a taper and some sculpturing wax. Use a yellow taper and from sculpturing wax cut a large, elongated heart. Cutting a paper pattern first would insure that you have the correct size. The tip of the petal should extend slightly beyond the tip of the taper. Wrap the large end of the petal around the candle 1″ or so from the base—high enough so it will just clear the top of candleholder. Position this part of the wax so that the petal flares out from the candle. Fasten with hot wax. Roll edges of petal outward and fasten part of petal to back of candle with hot wax. Use half regular wax and half sculpturing wax to keep the petal from drooping. Cut leaves if desired and attach to bottom of flower.

Ham Can Candle

A ham can makes an unusual mold and the cans come in an assortment of sizes. However, a ham can is not one of the usual upright molds, and it must be poured while mold is resting on its side. This means that the normal method of wicking will not work with this type of mold. A hot ice pick can be utilized for making a wick hole after candle is removed from the mold and wick then threaded through this hole.

Another method is to pour the candle in two sections. Pour the mold half full of hot wax and refill once. When wax is firm, place a wick in the center of candle and fasten by brushing with hot wax. Where the top of the wick and top of mold meet, press wick against side of can and bring it over the cut edge of the can. Fasten with a clothes pin or paper clip. A small amount of rubber cement or floral adhesive will aid in keeping the wick flush with the side of the can. Pour the other half of the mold and, this time, don't refill. By not refilling, you will have an indentation in what will be the front of the candle. The indentation will present more possibilities for decorating than a flat surface would.

When candle is removed from the mold, you will find that the wick is embedded in the wax. Pull the wick from the wax so

Illustration No. 36. Ham-can candle and Easter Madonna.

it stands upright and fill in the small hole left by the wick with hot wax the same color as the candle.

The cross on the candle in Illustration No. 36 was cut from a sheet of wax and decorated with hand-molded calla lilies. A small angel and a group of calla lilies complete the decoration.

Madonna

A wax or plastic Madonna and some plastic calla lilies can convert a plain square candle into one that reflects the true feeling of Easter. (Illustration No. 36.) This is one of those candles that belies the amount of effort it takes to make it. The wax-dipped lilies are put on in a matter of seconds with straight pins and the Madonna attached with hot wax or a combination of wires and hot wax.

By using poinsettias, holly, or pine branches instead of calla lilies, it can become a Christmas candle.

Mother's Day

Any candle that would please Mom would be an appropriate candle for Mother's Day. There are foil decorations that spell

"Mother" and these can be placed on a decorated candle to more specifically tie it in with Mother's Day. Pictures of members of the family glued or pinned to a candle would be cherished by some mothers. However, a candle appropriately decorated to fit the decor of the home of the recipient would be very acceptable for a Mother's Day gift.

Father's Day

I'm afraid the number of men who would be delighted with the gift of a candle is considerably less than the number of women. There are some men who really like candles and for these men on Father's Day, the following decorations would be appropriate. Anything that depicts Father's hobby—from fishing flies to bowling pins. The cake decorating houses have small decorations for almost any sport or hobby imaginable and these can be used as the basis for a Father's Day candle. Another idea is to cut a tie and collar from sheets of wax. Place the tie down the front of a candle and wrap the collar around the top of the candle, fastening both with hot wax. Stripes or wild designs can be painted on the tie.

Fourth of July

Often Independence Day is celebrated with an outdoor cookout. A good candle for such an occasion is a layered red, white, and blue candle poured in a glass container. The glass surrounding the flame will reduce the likelihood of its being blown out by some stray gust of wind. If you need an indoor candle, try decorating with little red birthday candles to represent firecrackers. Lay out a row of candles long enough to circle a large candle and thread two pieces of small twine, through the candles. Have one piece of twine going over each candle and the other piece passing under the candle. Brush the twine with hot wax after it has been placed around all the candles and then fasten the string of "firecrackers" around a large candle. If you want realism in your candle, remove the powder from some small firecrackers and use them for decoration. Small flags would also be very appropriate as a candle decoration for this occasion.

Football

While the football season can't really be classified as a holiday, it doesn't fit any of the other classifications in this book either. However, since we have worked up to fall, I am including it in this section. You may spend the rest of your life without feeling that you must make a football candle. Then again, you may be having an after-the-game party where such a candle would be the ultimate touch. As your fame as a candlemaker increases, you could be called upon to decorate for a football banquet.

The quickest candle to make is one decorated with the good, old standby—artificial flowers. A combination of school colors and plastic mums makes a football decoration that's hard to top.

If you are ever asked to decorate for a football banquet, a very effective and comment-causing centerpiece can be made without too much effort. A large rectangle of styrofoam can be the football field. Pour four skinny round candles for the goalposts. Wrap these candles in strips of colored wax poured in the needed school colors. Cut two holes the size of the candles and about a half an inch deep in each end of the styrofoam, and place candles in these holes. Dig holes in the sides of the candle goal posts and insert small wooden dowels between each set of posts, fastening with hot wax. These dowels may also be wrapped with strips of colored wax. Outline the playing area between the goalposts with strips of plastic tape and position two football teams on the field. Football players may be obtained from cake decorating houses. Finish the centerpiece by wrapping ribbon in the school colors around the outside edge of the styrofoam.

Little football candles made from small plastic football molds could easily solve the problem of the favors to be placed at each plate.

Halloween

It will be hard to replace the cut-out pumpkin head as the favorite Halloween light of the small fry, but a candle trimmed with ghosts, witches, goblins, black cats, or other symbols of Halloween will certainly intrigue them.

A jack-o-lantern candle can be made by using a fluted salad mold and joining the two halves together. Paint on a face. If

Illustration No. 37. Halloween and Thanksgiving.

you would like a hollow jack-o-lantern to be used with a votive candle, pour two halves of a fluted mold but pour out the liquid wax after a shell of sufficient thickness has formed. Join the two halves with hot wax and cut eyes, nose, and a mouth in the shell. Also cut a hole in the top so the heat from the candle flame won't cause the top of candle to melt.

The candle in Illustration No. 38 was decorated with easy-to-make pumpkins, hat, and broom. The pumpkins were poured in a small plastic mold and the hat and broom cut from sculpturing wax. Use a knife or fork to make indentations in the broom head to resemble straw.

Thanksgiving

Almost any candle in a rich fall color decorated with autumn leaves, chrysanthemums, or other fall flowers is perfect for a Thanksgiving decoration. If you prefer the symbols of Thanksgiving on your candle, the turkey would head the list. Plastic or molded Pilgrims or Pilgrim hats and guns made of wax would also leave no doubt that the candle belongs to the Thanksgiving season.

For the candle in Illustration No. 38, a turkey and fruit spilling from a cornucopia depict the bounty of Thanksgiving. The fruit and turkey are from a wax mold and the cornucopia, or horn of plenty, is made from a triangle of sculpturing wax. Fold the ends of the triangle together, seal with hot wax, and bend the end of the horn into an upward curve. Small straw cornucopias are often available during the Thanksgiving season and they make wonderful candle decorations.

Christmas

And now we come to the last and best holiday of the year. Only the Scrooges find no joy in Christmas time. From the youngest to the eldest the excitement, the sharing, the festivities, and goodwill toward men seems to make each of us a little better person.

Candlecrafters look forward to this time of the year with mixed feelings. They know that now is when their candles are most in demand and for many it is a race against time to fill all the orders. Yet even with the rush and lack of time, Christmas candles are the most satisfying ones to make.

Believe it or not, some people start their Christmas candles in January and work on them in spare moments during the year. These are the people who can face the last hectic weeks before Christmas with a serenity that infuriates the rest of us who have procrastinated until the last minute. Other people work better under pressure and secretly enjoy the frantic pace they must maintain to finish ahead of the calendar in the headlong race toward December 25th.

For those procrastinators the first few Christmas candles described will be ones that can be put together in a hurry.

Poinsettias

Plastic poinsettias—large, small and in between—are life-savers for harried Christmas candlemakers. In just a few minutes they can handsomely convert a plain candle into one that fairly shouts "Christmas." In Illustration No. 38 three large poinsettias were sprinkled with glitter and quickly inserted in the candle by using the old indispensable icepick. The same method

Illustration No. 38. Quickie Christmas candles.

was used to fasten the small poinsettias and pine clusters to the other candle. The holly leaves were pinned to the candle before the poinsettias were inserted in the holes. Each candle was finished in less than five minutes.

Christmas Balls

Another quickie is made with Christmas balls and a tree ornament. Dump whipped wax on the candle and place two rows of different colored balls in a circle in the wax. In the center place a larger Christmas tree ornament, sprinkle the whipped wax with glitter and you have another candle that can be squeezed into your dwindling time. (Illustration No. 38.)

This candle version can be varied endlessly. Small figurines, Christmas tree beads, small Christmas decorations of all kinds can be pressed into whipped wax for an easy-to-assemble candle.

In Illustration No. 39 three gold plastic angels were pushed into a base of whipped wax, resulting in a candle that belies the small amount of decorating time spent on it.

Illustration No. 39. Christmas angels and whipped wax for a candle to assemble in minutes.

Reindeer Candle

From here on the Christmas candles become a little more elaborate and time consuming. The reindeer candle in Illustration No. 40 combines pink and silver for a glittering unreal, but attractive, snow scene. A five point salad mold was used for the base and after it was attached to the dark pink candle, it was covered with pale pink whipped wax. The little reindeer were sprayed silver and sprinkled with silver glitter. Silver Christmas beads strung on wire were placed in the whipped wax and arranged against the side of candle. Reindeer were pressed into the whipped wax on each point and the whipped wax sprinkled with silver glitter.

Pine branches, holly leaves, or small poinsettias could be substituted for the Christmas beads. The points could hold small Santa Clauses, angels, or other Christmas figures instead of the deer.

Santa Head

Practically everyone who has ever made candles is familiar with the Santa head made in a cone mold and eyebrows, moustache, beard, and fur made with whipped wax. This Santa head is merely a variation of that theme. The Santa in Illustration No. 40 still uses the whipped wax for the fur on his hat, but sculpturing wax is utilized for the other parts. Eyebrows and moustache were cut from a sheet of wax and fastened to the face with hot wax. The beard consists of three semi-circles of wax that have been slashed with scissors. Each of these cut pieces of wax is curled. The bottom half circle is attached first, then the middle, and finally the top one. The beard can be made fuller by making more slashes, making curls tighter, and by adding more rows of wax.

Wise Man

A tall round taper mold or the cone mold are equally good for this candle and each mold alters the appearance of the candle. The tall round taper produces a tall slender Wise Man and the cone mold turns out one that is shorter and fatter. Illustration No. 41 shows a Wise Man made by using the taper mold. When candle is poured, leave a long wick so wick can be threaded through the head.

Pour head in the small ball mold and after it is removed

Illustration No. 40. Reindeer and Santa.

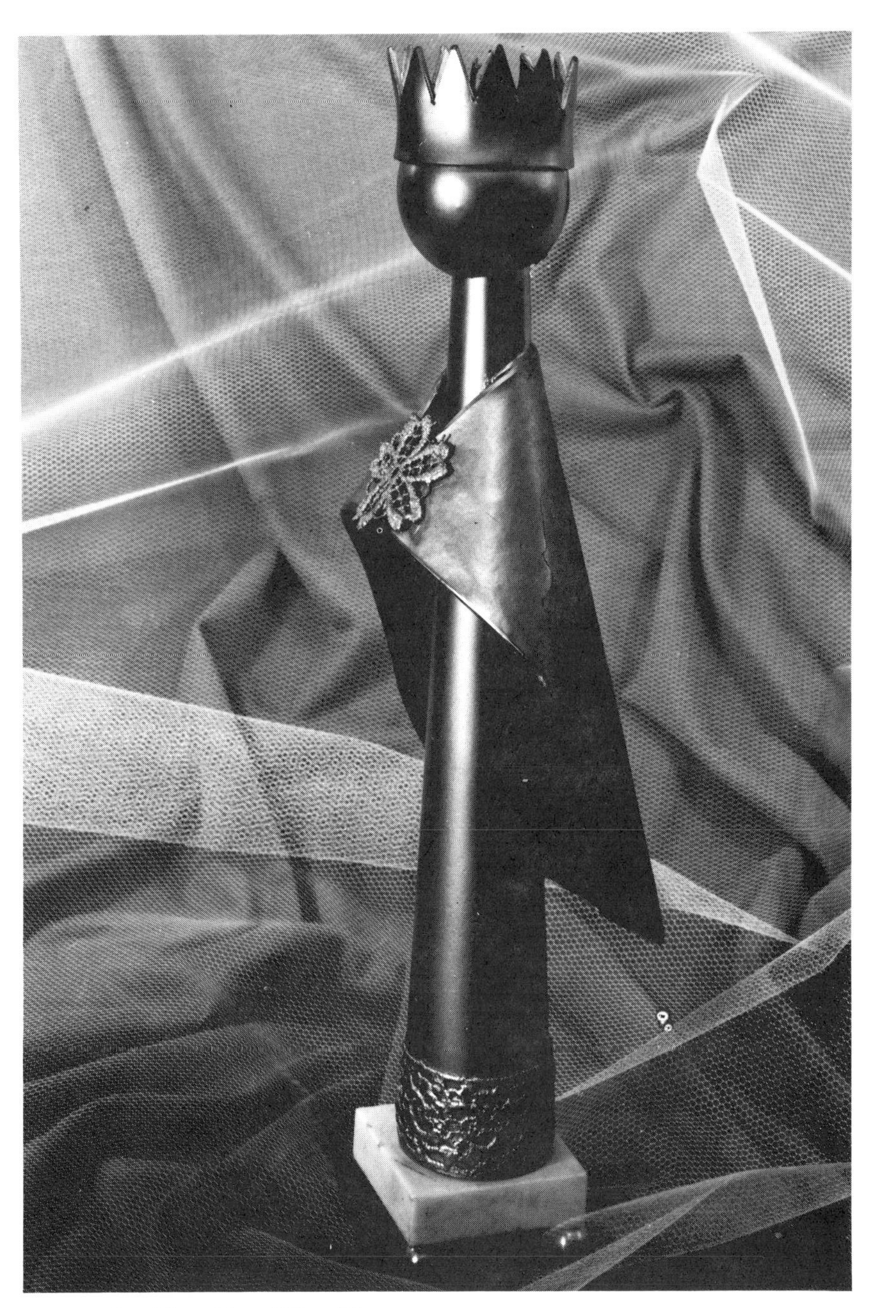

Illustration No. 41. Wise Man.

from mold, cut a hole in the ball large enough for the top of candle to fit into. With a hot icepick, punch a hole through the head, thread the wick through this hole, plug the hole around the wick with clay, and pour a little hot wax into the large hole in the ball. Turn candle upside down and push it into the hole in the ball. When wax has cooled slightly, pull wick taut. Leave candle upside down until wax has solidified enough so it won't run down the side of candle. Cut a cape from a sheet of sculpturing wax and wrap it around the top of candle. Fasten with hot wax. With hot wax fasten a piece of heavy lace around the bottom of candle and attach a lace medallion to front of cape to cover the evidences of the hot wax used for sealing the cape to the candle. Cut rectangle from sheet of wax and use your scissors or a sharp knife to cut the points. After the points have been cut in the crown, place it on top of the head and fasten with hot wax. The entire candle can be sprayed gold or silver if desired.

This candle can be made as plain as the one illustrated or it can be made much more ornate by the addition of jewels, braid, gold cord designs, etc. to the skirt and cape.

Package Candle

Gaily wrapped packages are such a part of the Christmas spirit, I feel that a package candle would be most appropriate. Pour a candle in large hurricane square mold, but make it a solid candle with a wick. Cut two long strips of wax from a sheet of soft wax and wrap one around the candle lengthwise and one crosswise, having them intersect in middle of candle. Don't forget to cut a hole in the strip that passes over the wick so the wick can be threaded through the hole instead of being squashed against the top of candle. Cut four short strips of wax and cut the ends to represent the ends of ribbon. Place these short strips at the four angles formed by the crisscrossed ribbon on the front of candle. Cut at least eight strips of wax and loop the ends together. Fasten these loops of wax to front of candle to form the bottom of bow. Cut shorter strips for the top row of the bow, loop the ends together and attach to front of candle just inside the bottom loops. Place pine clusters, Christmas balls, etc. in the center of bow. Ribbon may be left as is or touched with gold or glitter. Little Christmas tags might be glued to candle to com-

Illustration No. 42. Christmas tree and package candle.

plete the illusion of a package. Fuller bows can be made by adding more ribbon loops. (Illustration No. 42.)

Mr and Mrs. Santa

In my opinion the star molds are the hardest of all to decorate. If you can't find something small enough to fit in between the points, you might as well be decorating a plain candle. In Illustration No. 43 a Mr. and Mrs. Santa Claus who could squeeze in between the points forms the basis for this decoration. Whipped wax was placed around the bottom of candle and brought up between the points. Mr. and Mrs. Santa were pushed into the wax between the points and small pine cones, pine clusters, and holly berries were stuck in the wax beneath and beside them. Whipped wax was dripped down from the top of candle and ridges touched with gold.

Half Candle

Half candles may be poured in bottles or in glass lamp chimneys as in Illustration No. 44. Cut a piece of cardboard to fit the inside of the glass container. The easiest way to do this is to measure around the outside of the glass with a piece of thin wire and then use the wire as a guide for cutting the cardboard. You will have a neater, more finished candle if you paint the bottom and sides of the cardboard the same color as the candle. Punch a hole in the center of cardboard, thread wick through the hole, and tie a knot in the end of wick beneath the cardboard. Push cardboard into container and pull wick taut. It may be necessary to pull on the wick with one hand and push and poke at the cardboard with a pencil or some object in order to get it lined up straight in the container. Put clear glue around the edges of the cardboard so it will stick to the container. Pull wick taut and tie it in place over a rod or pencil placed across the top of container. When glue dries, fill container from cardboard up with hot wax.

When using a lamp chimney, the decorations may be arranged in the bottom half of the chimney and the chimney then pushed into a styrofoam base. For this candle a plastic angel, poinsettias, and holly leaves were used as decoration. Pine clusters were pushed into the base of styrofoam.

When this half candle is poured in a bottle, the decorations

Illustration No. 43. Sculpture wax angels and Mr. & Mrs. Santa.

Illustration No. 44. Half Candle.

must be arranged in the bottom of bottle before the cardboard is glued in place.

Angel

The cone mold was used for this candle and the medium ball mold for the head. The head is attached to the body in the same manner as the Wise Man candle. Cut two triangles of soft wax and fold ends together to make the sleeves. Cut two elongated oval shapes and fasten these hands inside the sleeves with hot wax. Bend the sleeves in the center and attach them to sides of body with hot wax. Cut a small rectangle of soft wax for the book and fold it in the center. Attach it to the hands of the angel. Using glitter in a tube, make a design for the collar and cuffs. Cut a large circle of soft wax and place it over the head of angel. Trim the circle so that bangs are formed with the hair hanging down the sides of face. Hair may be turned up in a flip or under in a pageboy. Roll a circle of wax and place it on top of the head for the halo. Paint on the mouth and eyebrows and cut two small rectangles. Slash the rectangle with scissors or knife, curve them upward slightly, form into a semi-circle, and glue on face for the eyelashes. Make wings of wax or paper foil and fasten to back of angel. (Illustration No. 45.)

Snowman

Plastic or metal ball molds are the easiest to use for making a snowman but bowls of different sizes will do very well if ball molds are not available. You will need a large, medium, and small mold. Each ball must be punched after it is poured and wick put in place. The wick will help hold the balls together but hot wax should also be used between each of the balls. Snowmen are usually covered with white whipped wax and the features can be painted on or bits of colored wax used to indicate features. The snowmen may be as simple or as elaborate as desired. Hats, scarves, brooms, pipes, etc. can be fashioned from sculpturing wax and added to dress up the snowman, or a pair of snow people could be made by putting an apron and hat on Mama.

Sculpture Wax Angels

The little angels in Illustration No. 43 can be made in any size. They are made by cutting a triangle for the skirt and fold-

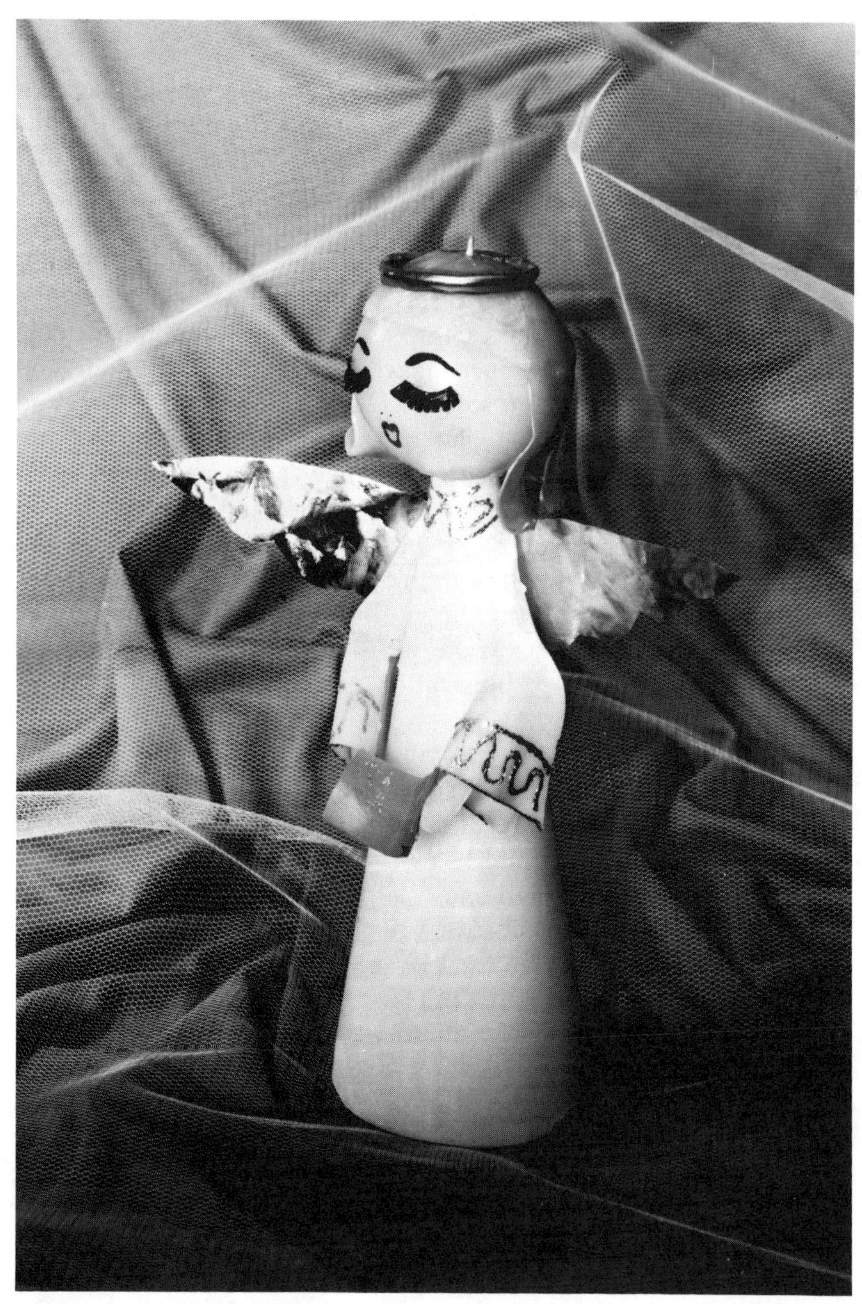

Illustration No. 45. Angel.

ing the two ends together. Cut off the tip of the triangle at the top. Cut two small triangles for the sleeves and fold these edges together. Fasten the sleeves to the cone body at the shoulders. Cut hands and slip inside the sleeves, fastening with hot wax. Bend the sleeves so hands are in a praying position. Outline sleeves and neck with glitter-in-a-tube. Cut small wings from sculpturing wax and fasten to back of angels. Dip small styrofoam balls in clear wax several times. Sticking a toothpick into the styrofoam and using the toothpick as a handle will make the dipping much easier. When balls are smooth, paint on faces and hair. Roll small circles of soft wax and attach to heads for halos. Paint the wings and halos gold. A small poinsettia was placed beneath each angel for added decoration.

Christmas Tree

To make the trunk of the cone-molded tree in Illustration No. 42 cut out both ends of a metal juice can, leaving a hollow round cylinder. Stand the can on a stove burner and leave it until it is very hot. Grasp the can with a hot pad and push the end that was on the burner into the center of bottom of candle. Let wax harden, then turn candle upside down and place it in a glass to hold it upright. Pour a small amount of hot wax into the can and let harden. This will prevent wax leakage when the can is filled with hot wax. When wax is hard, fill can about half full of hot wax and let this cool.

Pour a fairly thick base and scoop out a shallow hole slightly larger than the end of can in the center of base. After this hole is made, drill or cut a small hole in the center of base all the way through. Place bottom end of can in scooped-out hole in base, and fill the hole with hot wax. When wax is hard, again turn candle upside down, place in glass, and through the small hole in base pour hot wax into the can until it reaches the top of hole in bottom of base. These wax pourings will tightly seal the trunk to the tree and base and keep it from becoming loose.

Cover candle with whipped wax and let cool. When wax is hard, pile mounds of whipped wax in rows around the candle, starting at the bottom. These piles of whipped wax will be the tree branches and they are more effective if they are staggered. When making the second row of branches, place them above and between the mounds on the first row and alternate these branches all the way up the side of the candle. As each branch is piled on the candle, insert a small Christmas ball at the bottom of the branch and sprinkle on glitter while the wax is still warm.

Cover the can with glue and coat thickly with glitter. Satin or velvet ribbon can also be wound around the can to disguise the fact that the trunk of this tree is really a juice can.

The base may need dipping to cover the joining of trunk and base.

Luminarias

Visitors to the Southwest during the Christmas season are invaribly awed by their first contact with luminarias. It is hard to believe that a brown paper bag containing some sand and a candle can create such a fantastic spectacle.

Albuquerque, New Mexico, calls itself "the most beautiful city in America on Christmas Eve" and this is no idle boast.

Illustration No. 46. Luminarias outlining walks and roof of a southwestern home.

The local resident never tire of the Christmas Eve luminaria displays and something would be missing from Christmas if they couldn't get in their cars and drive through the city to look at these lovely lights. There is also an annual guided luminaria tour by bus for visitors to Albuquerque and these tourists have spread the fame of the "candle-in-a-bag" all over the United States.

The origin of luminarias has been lost in antiquity and there are different versions of how they came into being. Some say luminarias derived from the shells of oil lighted by the Moors of Spain during festive occasions. Supposedly the Spanish descendents of the Conquistadores introduced the custom of the "little fires" on Christmas Eve. Another theory is that these lights were borrowed from the Tortugas Indians.

The first lights were small bonfires placed in front of homes to guide the Christ Child to shelter. Worshipers on their way to midnight mass would also find their way lighted by fires lining the dusty road to church. Later piñon was stacked on the tops of adobe houses and walls, and when a signal was given on Christmas Eve all the fires were lighted at the same time.

When the freight wagons came from Mexico bringing china dishes for the wealthy, these dishes were wrapped in layers of silklike, transparent papers. The fiesta-loving Spanish women fashioned this paper into different shapes, placed sand and a candle inside, and used them to light their festivals. About one hundred years ago traders brought the brown paper bags to New Mexico and these inexpensive bags provided the solution to the problem of protecting the candles from the ever-present wind.

Colored Christmas lights eventually replaced the luminarias and the sack candles were used only in the rural areas without electricity. A fraternity at the University of New Mexico is credited with bringing the luminarias back into vogue. The fraternity wanted to enter a Christmas lighting contest but had no money for decorations. One of the members told of seeing the sack candles in some of the small villages and the boys agreed to decorating with luminarias. They made their lights, placed them around the fraternity house, and easily won first place in the contest.

Rows of luminarias can be used along walks, driveways, walls, and rooftops. The displays are most effective when a whole neigh-

Illustration No. 47. Luminarias spreading their glow along walks and around a pool.

borhood collaborates and everyone decorates his home with these lights. No other outside lighting should be used as it detracts from the incredible beauty of the flickering luminarias. Some large homes, churches, and commercial buildings will have thousands of these sack candles lighting their property.

Aside from the spectacle of the lights, one of the most noticeable traits of a luminaria neighborhood is the absolute stillness. Cars are driven slowly, no horns are honked and there are no squealing brakes. Even in a closed car there is a tendency to converse in whispers.

Luminaria parties are a common occurrence in the Southwest during the Christmas season. Friends and neighbors are invited to help fold and fill the sacks and enjoy the good food and drink of Christmas time.

Many youth groups make money for their clubs and churches by selling luminarias to people who don't have the time or desire to make their own. Orders are taken a week or two in advance and on Christmas Eve the luminarias are delivered and set in place.

To make a luminaria use a size 8 or 10 brown paper grocer's bag. Fold the rim of the bag down two times for firmness against the wind and to hold the sack away from the candle. Fill a one pound coffee can full of sand and pour it into the bottom of sack. Push a short, fat candle which will not tip over into the sand in the bottom of the sack. These glowing sack candle decorations of Spain and Old Mexico are lighted at dusk on Christmas Eve and allowed to burn until the candles are extinguished by the sand. (Illustrations Nos. 46 and 47.)

7

THE BUSINESS END OF CANDLES

REQUESTS to buy your candles will follow the perfecting of your candlecrafting skills. No other sale will ever be as exciting or confidence-building as that first one. Although you feel your work can stand a critical comparison, to have that feeling confirmed by a customer anxious to exchange her money for your candle makes all the spilled wax and frustrations worthwhile.

Some people invest time and money learning candlecrafting because they like to explore new horizons or expand their knowledge. A period of pleasant relaxation or the thrill of creativity is reward enough.

For others the primary reason for becoming involved with wax in the first place was monetary. There is no decision to be made about retaining their amateur standing or turning professional as additional income was their goal from the beginning.

Initial sales are usually made to friends and relatives and the candles are drastically underpriced. There is a general tendency to be hesitant about charging a friend as much for a candle as you would a stranger. Perhaps you feel that you would be making candles anyway because you enjoy it and these prices will pay for your materials. This is a generous attitude, but not very businesslike. There may be no desire on your part to be businesslike or make a profit, in which case selling for cost or a little above will help defray the expense of making candles for sheer pleasure.

If you have any thoughts of going commercial, beware of making the mistake of underpricing your candles to lure those first customers. It's far easier to lower the price of a candle that doesn't move than it is to raise prices on all your candles when you realize there isn't any profit. If you offer quality and beauty, you will find plenty of customers willing to pay a fair price for your candles.

Candles can't be burned as fast as enthusiastic candlecrafters can make them, and it's sometimes smart to give away your surplus until you are completely sure of your abilities. If this is done, improper burning, falling decorations or other problems that take time to master will not mean a dissatisfied customer. The better pottery factories smash their imperfect pieces to bits and throw them away rather than sell them as seconds and have their names associated with an inferior product. Some candle companies could take a lesson from them.

If you plan even a limited mail order business, try several different methods of packaging and ship the candles to your out-of-town friends. Ask them to let you know the condition of the candles upon arrival at their destination. In this way you will learn which candles can stand the rigors of shipping and the best packaging methods. Your customers won't be stuck with filing a series of damage claims because of your lack of knowledge.

Starting small and growing gradually is a success formula with much merit. Even with a large amount of capital to invest, a small home business is usually the best place to start. This, of course, would not apply to those with previous experience in managing a successful gift shop or something similar. Such a background would give these people the training, practice and business know-how to be reasonably sure of what they were doing.

A shop in your home will make changes in your daily life and thought should be given to these changes. The active participation of your family in this new venture can be very helpful, but their cooperation is vital if the harmony of the home is to be retained. A rush order can make meals late or nonexistent. There may be interruptions in the family routine from thoughtless customers who feel that because home and business are combined, your working hours are anytime from daylight to midnight. These inconveniences can cause a strain in households where privacy and punctuality are important.

In addition to your usual chores of cooking, cleaning, baby sitting, chauffeuring, etc., you will also find you are a bookkeeper, cashier, sales clerk, stock clerk, purchasing agent, office manager, public relations manager, advertising agency, artist, and janitor; in other words, a one-man or woman business.

If all this doesn't discourage you—and it usually doesn't—you are ready for the next step. Try to arrange a full day for visiting all the departments and filling out all the forms that are necessary to get you started on a sound and legal footing.

The first stop is the zoning department in your town to be sure you will be allowed to conduct a business in your home. Since a candle shop will not detract from the neighborhood, cause unpleasant odors, or create a public nuisance, no difficulty should be encountered. However, in some residential areas restrictions are so stringent that a shop would be downright illegal, and the time to find out is before your shop is in operation.

The tightest restrictions are likely to be on the type of sign you will be permitted to display for advertising your shop. Regulations may govern the size and type of sign as well as its location. In my neighborhood no signs can be placed outside the house. A sign in the window is permissible if it is inside. Zoning ordinances in each town are different and the only way to be sure of what you can or can't do is to check with the zoning department.

Once you have the approval of the zoning board, go to the city license bureau and find out what licenses are required by this department. A business license may not be necessary for a shop in your own home but the wisest course is to find out from an official source.

The name of your shop should also receive serious consideration. Most towns require that businesses operating under an assumed name file an affidavit stating the owner's name and address. The city clerk often handles these registrations or can tell you who to contact.

Any name other than your own is considered an assumed name and the usual form of registration is "John Doe doing business as The Candle Shop." Having the name of your business on file will allow anyone needing to contact you to find your correct address.

If you want to register your assumed name to prevent its use by another person, there is an additional fee for this service. Registration is recommended only if the name of the business is so unusual or catchy that it would tempt someone with less imagination.

Your state probably has a sales tax law, in which case you will need a state license. Records must be kept for tax purposes and tax paid according to law. City sales taxes are being adopted by more and more municipalities. If there is such a law in your town, find out what its regulations are. A sales tax license will enable you to buy from wholesalers without paying tax on your purchases. It is also probable that if you only sell wholesale you would not have to pay the tax.

Now that all the forms and applications have been filled out and your licenses are in order, you can start planning your shop. It can be a section of one room, an unused bedroom, a converted garage or, if you're lucky, a basement. The display area should be made as attractive as possible without investing too much money in fixtures. Painted shelving made of heavy lengths of planks with cinder block or brick used for supports and dividers is relatively inexpensive. Secondhand or discarded end or lamp tables are often just the right size to spotlight a prized candle or two.

Plan your display area with ample walking-around space so customers won't be nervous about knocking a candle off a table or shelf. Glass display cases will protect your candles, but the sense of touch is as important to most shoppers as what they see and they like to run their fingers down the sides of a glassy candle. Display area and storage and working area should be separated if at all possible, even if only by a curtain.

To more efficiently organize your storage area, put as many decorating materials as possible in plastic bags and hang them on the wall. If space is really limited, they can even be hung from the ceiling. Hang the bags with elastic rather than wire or cord so you can walk under them without bumping your head. Tie a loop in the end of the elastic, wrap one end of a piece of wire around the opening of a plastic bag, and bend a hook in the other end. A stick with a bent nail on the end or a coathanger can be used to catch the loop in the elastic and pull it down from the ceiling far enough to insert the wire hook. When elastic is released, the bag will pop up out of the way till needed again.

If pricing has been a hit or miss proposition, the time is now for establishing a firm policy. It's impossible to give directions for pricing candles because so many factors enter into this puzzling job. Candles sold in a small town won't bring the prices that the same candles would in a large city. Someone with a good location in a tourist area will be better reimbursed than the candle-crafter on a farm.

Visit any candle shops near you and check on how their candles are marked. You can fairly accurately estimate the cost of decorating materials and the amount of time involved to arrive at a close guess as to the markup. This is the favorite sport of candlecrafters, so don't be bashful. The owners of these shops will be making comparisons in your establishment one of these days.

Regardless of how much pleasure you derive from making candles, if you go into business you want to make money. Therefore, you must price your candles to cover the cost of material, overhead (utilities, rent, advertising, etc.), and your time. There is also depreciation on your molds, particularly plaster and plastic, to be figured in this cost.

Arriving at the time spent decorating a candle is relatively simple, but your candlemaking time is more complicated. Computing this time from pouring of candle to removal from mold is unrealistic as you will be doing many other things while wax is heating and cooling. Make a test of how long it takes to break up wax and put it in the melting pot, how much time for pouring and refilling. How little time is actually spent making a candle will probably surprise you. Plan your time efficiently—while wax is heating, decorate a candle. After you put it in the water bath, decorate another one.

When you have determined how long it takes to make a candle from a block of wax to finished piece, set a price on your labor. Add the cost of your labor, cost of all materials used, and enough to cover overhead and depreciation. This will be the actual cost of your candle. The markup over this cost will be your profit.

Your markup will be partially dependent on the beauty and originality of the candle and price you can expect to obtain in your area. Exceptionally lovely candles in exclusive shops sometime sell for $50.00 to $100.00 and it is unlikely that more than $10.00 worth of material could be in these candles. The artistry and skill of the creator are being sold in such instances. These prices are exceptions and candles tagged from $2.50 to $10.00 are more likely to find a buyer in the small shop.

Build your business gradually, studying each phase of it and learning as you progress. The first year or two most of the profits should go back into the business in the form of more molds and better equipment.

Limited quantity production can be initiated without sacrificing quality. If profits warrant, replace the coffee pots with a secondhand deep fat fryer with a spout. Some are available that will maintain a constant temperature for hours. Have a sheet metal shop make a water bath container that will hold eight or ten candles instead of one or two. With improved equipment such as this, a dozen candles can be made in approximately the same time as one or two were made without it.

Use your capital to stock up at sales. Christmas decorations in January are a drug on the market and the prices are lowered drastically to avoid having to carry the stock over for another year. By buying marked-down items at after-season sales you not only save money but will have the things you need for decorating in advance of a given season. For instance, by buying Christmas decorations in January, you can start making your Christmas candles in July if you wish and not have to wait until the stores begin to stock Christmas items in the winter.

The list of candle suppliers is limited now, but as the home candle business grows, so will the number of suppliers. Quantity buying is a good way to save money, if—and there are several ifs. Order in small quantities from an unknown supplier until you decide whether quality and service warrant larger orders. Quantity buying is advisable only if you have the capital to invest in the long haul and the space necessary for storing a large stock.

Some items, such as paints, tend to dry out and hard, caked bottles or tubes of paint that sat on the shelf too long mean money out of your pocket.

On the plus side, quantity buying can save you money by taking advantage of discounts. Shipping charges on one large package from a single source are usually less expensive than several smaller parcels from various areas around the country. You also save time in your bookkeeping, ordering, and checking when package is received. It is less time consuming to report one damaged shipment than several. One letter about delayed shipments can be written more quickly than four or five. There is an old saying that "time is money" and in the case of candlecrafting, the less time you can spend on bookkeeping details the more time you can spend making candles to exchange for money.

Basic items will be offered by all suppliers and there are advantages to limiting your orders to a small number of suppliers rather than giving a portion of your business to all of them. The order of a regular customer, even if the order is not large, will be given preferred handling over the one from an unknown buyer. Establishing friendly relations with your suppliers is good business and can pay dividends in terms of credit, special service, and often in expert advice on some business problem.

Shipping charges are big items for the retailer. Once you have established your primary sources of supply, study all the transportation facilities available to you. Compare parcel post and express rates with charges by different truck lines in your area. Bus lines often offer fast service and cheaper rates, so don't forget them. Make a chart of the distance from your suppliers and the cost of shipping various weights via the different companies. By doing this, you can determine the least expensive and ask the supplier to ship accordingly.

In a home business it is imperative that you set your store hours and stick to them. This is necessary for you and for the customer. The customer has a right to expect that you will be available during the hours your business is supposed to be open and you have a right to some privacy after the business day is over. You needn't sit in the shop all day waiting for a customer, but be close enough so that if one does come you will know it. Be polite, but firm, about selling candles when the shop is closed; otherwise, your business hours will be meaningless.

Now that you have set up shop, how do you spread the word? Spot announcements on T.V., an ad in the newspaper, or direct mail advertising are all expensive. One form of advertising that will cost you nothing is word-of-mouth. Tell everyone you know that you are in the candle business and ask them to tell their friends to come by and look around.

An open house can be one of the best stimulants for a retail business. A telephone call or handwritten note can be used for an invitation. You might state that the open house is to introduce your new shop and give people an opportunity to browse and no candles will be sold until a later date. This will attract people who might be hesitant because they would feel obligated to buy. Refreshments of coffee and cookies or something similar should be served if finances permit. Many of the onlookers will probably be back to buy when you have your official opening.

Newspapers are always looking for feature stories and a few paragraphs about your fledging business would be valuable free advertising. Let your local paper know about your open house. It is possible they would be interested enough to send a reporter to cover it.

Giving away a few candles can often be an inexpensive advertising bonanza. Donate some candles to a charity bazaar but request that you be allowed to place a small sign nearby stating the candles were donated by your candle shop. Watch the newspapers and when there is an article about a club luncheon or dinner, call the decorating chairman. Offer to decorate the tables with candles in exchange for an announcement that candles were provided by your shop.

Exhibit your work at every opportunity. Craft shows, state and county fairs, or a booth at a bazaar; all offer opportunities to bring your candles to the attention of a large number of potential customers. Have printed cards or even slips of paper containing your shop name and address available for those interested. Inexpensive candles are best sellers at these places, but in the background have some of your more elaborate pieces to show what you are capable of doing.

You think you can't stand up in front of a large group and give a talk? You can with a candle in your hand. Giving a demonstration is considerably different from looking your audience in the eye and presenting a speech. Demonstrations are quite simply explaining the details of making and decorating candles and showing your audience the various steps involved. No prepared speech is necessary; in fact, it's undesirable.

Because of the time element involved, demonstrations rely heavily on decoration. The exception is the container candle. Although the wax may not be hard by the time the demonstration is over, the audience has been taken through all the steps necessary for making a container candle.

How demonstrations are handled depends on the demonstrator, and each one has a different approach. For those of you who would like to give a demonstration and are uncertain as to how to proceed, I will give you a very broad and general view of the manner in which I handle them. Two or three demonstrations will smooth out the rough spots and show you what to add or eliminate for a more interesting program.

A week or so before the demonstration, make a written list of all the supplies and equipment you will need to take with you. Double check this list the day before the event to be certain everything is included. A few minutes spent on this detail may save you the embarrassment of apologizing to the audience because something vital was left at home. I learned this the hard way when I was before a large crowd and found I hadn't brought along everything I should have.

After a few opening remarks about candles, an explanation is given of the functions of wax, stearic, and crystals and how they are combined to make a candle. Small amounts of each are displayed so the audience will understand just what is being discussed. A metal mold is then wicked and a complete "dry run" is made of all the steps to be followed in making a candle.

The "dry-run" is for me the most satisfactory way of showing how a candle is made because of the long period of time necessary between pouring wax into a mold and removing the completed candle. I usually take along a candle still in the mold and show how it is removed and finished.

Candles and decorating materials are brought along and the candles decorated with explanations being given for each step. Decorating can include attaching flowers and leaves with pins and/or ice pick method, fastening sequins and braid, painting or even a quick lesson in hand molding wax flowers. I like to pour a small ceramic mold and let the audience see all the steps from pouring to removing and finally, attaching to candle. A small container candle can be decorated and then poured so they can see the actual making of a candle.

Description of candlemaking and the decorating of three candles usually takes approximately an hour to an hour and a half and then a question and answer period follows. Demonstrations can be as long or short as desired by you and the audience. It's a good policy to have an extra candle or two to decorate in the event you complete your planned schedule faster than anticipated.

It's more fun for you and the audience if an informal atmosphere is maintained. Encourage them to question anything they don't understand during the demonstration. If you don't know the answer to one of the questions asked—don't improvise. Admit you don't know the answer. If you were skilled in every phase and facet of the candlemaking art you would be drawing fancy fees as a consultant rather than giving a small demonstration.

Club groups are always hungry for new programs and you could probably schedule all the demnostrations your time would permit. Some people do these for nothing in order to become known and others charge a small fee. In any event, always take some decorated candles to sell if anyone wants to buy.

If demonstrations become a way of life with you, why not set up a kit containing all the items needed for demonstrating? Keep this kit separated from your regular candle equipment and you can grab your kit and be ready to go on a moment's notice. The time saved packing supplies will be worth the cost of extra equipment.

In addition to adding to the potential list of prospective customers for your finished candles, your demonstrations will inspire some of the onlookers to make their own candles. They may ask if you would sell them a mold and enough material for one candle. Your first and normal reaction would be—why should I encourage them to compete with me? This is something you can't fight; if they are interested enough they will find their supplies somewhere else. So if you can't sell them a candle, sell the supplies they need. This can be as profitable as the sale of candles and much less work.

You make your profit on supplies by buying wholesale and selling retail and again your friendly supplier can come to your aid. Write and ask about becoming a dealer in your area. In fact, write to several suppliers to find out which ones will offer the best dealer discounts. Concentrate mostly on molds and candlemaking supplies. If you have access to unusual decorating items, by all means put them on your shelves. However, it's not good business to tie up your money in decorating supplies that are carried by a dozen other stores in your area.

Leftover wax can be poured into small loaf pans and sold to people who want only a pound or two of wax. Customers are often delighted to find the wax already colored and/or scented and an additional charge should be made for this service.

Try not to waste anything. If there isn't enough wax remaining after your candles are completed to resell in a block, use what is left to make scented votive candles or floaters. Place these in a conspicuous place for the impulse buyer. Packaging several in a plastic bag to retail for about a dollar might be more profitable than selling the items separately. The little candles not only turn excess wax scraps into good sellers, but they also solve the problem of what to do with the bits and pieces of wick left over from making larger candles.

Something else to consider is the sale of plain candles for the customers who would like to have a go at decorating but have no desire to buy the equipment to make candles or get involved in pouring wax. Some brief instructions on applying decorations should be given at time of sale. If, after a certain period of time, the candles are still on your shelf, decorate them yourself and sell them as decorated candles.

Business hours curtail your personal freedom and for the free soul who doesn't relish being confined at home all day, teaching candlecrafting can provide extra money and let you chose the hours you wish to work.

A converted garage, basement, or even a large kitchen will serve as a classroom. Limit the size of class to a number that can be handled easily. I think ten students would be an absolute maximum and less would probably be better. No matter how much you stress the possibility of burns and the safe way to handle hot wax, you will find some of your students so careless it will scare you witless.

A typed or mimeographed sheet given to students at the beginning of each series of lessons will avoid the possibility of misunderstandings. This list might contain fee to be charged, class hours, number of classes per session, materials to be furnished by you and by the student, and clean-up expected.

An alarm clock set for fifteen minutes before the end of class will warn students not to get started on any lengthy project and also alert them to the fact that clean-up must be started soon. Unless you insist on each student cleaning up his working area, you will likely find this job is considered all yours.

If space in your home is not available for classes, go out to teach. Clubs are likely propects and the Y is always anxious to find qualified teachers of any craft. Scout groups and churches are often interested in learning candlemaking for money-raising projects.

When I teach away from home, I furnish the molds and nothing else. Students are given a list of materials needed for candlemaking and asked to bring whatever they want for decorating. You would need a truck to haul all your supplies if you tried to furnish everything.

In every class there will be a student who asks to take a mold home and pour some candles before the next lesson. My stock answer to this request is "I am sure you would take care of the mold, but because of some unfortunate experiences in the past, I have had to make a rule never to loan my molds."

Have definite regulations about visitors, whether classes are in or out of your home. Perhaps once during a class, preferably a decorating session, students could bring along interested guests. They might be intrigued enough to become your students the next time you offer lessons. Nothing, however, can disrupt and disorganize a class so quickly as people with nothing specific to do milling around chatting with the students and bombarding you with questions.

Another rule should be no children. Curious fingers and hot wax are a dangerous combination and it will be impossible for you to watch all that is going on. You will have your hands full at first keeping the adults out of trouble.

Fees may be handled in different ways. A flat rate might be charged for the lessons with all materials being bought separately. If you furnish some or all of the materials, try to get them wholesale and add enough markup to make a profit.

Or you could offer a package deal—so many candles for a set price. In this case you would be expected to furnish everything needed for making and decorating candles, and a limit would have to be set on the type and amount of decorating materials allowed for each candle.

If lessons are to be given in the home, check with your insurance agent to find out if your coverage will include any accidents that might occur during a lesson. Accidents are not too likely, but you will sleep better if you know the possibility is covered.

Maybe you are one of the people who has only a limited amount of time that can be spent on candles. Or perhaps you only make candles when you are in a candlemaking mood. Then there are those to whom retail selling, teaching, or demonstrating doesn't appeal at all. If you fall into this group, and you feel that your candles have sales appeal, perhaps selling wholesale would be your field.

Basically, this is just a matter of finding a retail outlet for your candles, collecting the money, and letting someone else worry about licenses, sales taxes, customers, etc. A good gift shop in your area would be the logical place to start. In the beginning you might have to place your candles on consignment. This means that you would leave your candles at a retail store and you would still have all the problems of breakage or damage. The management would assume no responsibility for them other than reasonable care. You would be paid for the candles as they are sold.

Often selling on consignment is the only way you can get your candles into a store. However, if they prove to be good sellers, you are in a better bargaining position, and at a later date you can insist that you be paid for each delivery of candles.

By adding a middleman (the retailer), you will not realize as much profit from your candles as you would if you retailed them yourself. The retailer must add his markup to your price and this markup is usually between 40% and 50%. An experienced retailer can estimate fairly accurately just how much he can charge for a certain object. If you prefer to make candles and sell them, without the attention to all the details necessary in a retail business, this would probably compensate for the lower profits.

Local success in selling your candles could mean that they would also sell successfully elsewhere. The next step would be to contact out-of-town stores to see if they would be interested in stocking your candles. Any out-of-town selling should be on a cash and not a consignment basis, as you have already determined that you are offering something with proven sales appeal.

The major problem will be packaging your candles so they

are not damaged during shipping. If there is a paper manufacturer anywhere in your area, take time to consult with them about packaging problems. They are experts in this field. Before sending any candles to your retail outlets, try several methods of packaging candles and ship them to friends in different parts of the country. This will quickly show you which is the best way. Ask your friends to report on the condition of the candles upon arrival.

And last, but very definitely not least—Income Tax. Records must be kept so you can figure your tax at the end of the year. These need not be detailed records, but they must be comprehensive enough so that if your books are ever audited you can satisfactorily prove your income and expenses to the Internal Revenue Service. Keep any receipts or cancelled checks showing money you have spent for your candlemaking operation. Sales slips, statements, or even deposit slips could be used to show the amount of money coming in.

If part of your house is used as a business, by all means check with the Internal Revnue Service to see what deduction you would be allowed for this use. A portion of your utilities can also be charged to the business.

As your business expands, it will likely be necessary to keep a set of books. For the small home beginning business, however, less exacting methods will suffice.

Twi-Lite Candles

A few years ago George and Irene Kinzie thought it would be fun to make their own Christmas candles. They bought some wax, made some candles and decorated them. Friends and relatives asked the Kinzies to make candles for them and they soon found themselves with a business as well as a hobby. When the Kinzies decided to approach candlemaking seriously, they realized there were some gaps in their knowledge of this craft and they spent some time in Denver learning the fundamentals of candlecrafting.

Col. Kinzie, a retired Air Force colonel, is in charge of the melting and coloring of the wax and the molding of the candles. Mrs. Kinzie puts the finishing touches on the molded candles, and when she is through with them no two are ever exactly alike.

Their "summer kitchen" was the base of operations when the Kinzies started their candlemaking. Here the pouring and

Illustration No. 48. George Kinzie pouring some of the famous Kinzie molds.

Illustration No. 49. Irene Kinzie removing a cut-glass candle from mold.

decorating was done. As they began to sell candles, they expanded to a display room just off the kitchen. This display room is now filled with candles of all colors and sizes. More orders meant a need for more space, and a larger workshop area was added; the "summer kitchen" was converted to a storage room for molds, and the wrapping and shipping department and a work area for making molds. The new workshop is used exclusively for the making and decorating of candles. Another addition is two more employees to help cope with the increased demand for their unique candles.

At the beginning of their candlemaking venture, the Kinzies made some molds from antique cut glass and now production of cut glass candles consumes most of their candlemaking hours. At present, the Kinzies have molds for 120 different designs of antique cut glass. Each summer they spend about six weeks touring the country looking for new cut glass designs to add to their line. They claim it is sometimes hard to determine whether their hobby is making candles or collecting antique glass.

In spite of the growing demand for their products, their candles are still painstakingly handcrafted and each candle receives individual attention. Although they have partially solved the problem of quantity production, they are completely uninterested in mass production. Each candle is slightly different from any other because of color depth, blending of colors, or the artistry of Irene Kinzie. They have found that to make one mold for a Twi-Lite candle requires a minimum of three days. Although their hobby has expanded into a business that furnishes candles to stores throughout the United States, their understanding with these shops is that Twi-Lite Candles will continue to supply candles only so long as they can be produced on a handcrafted basis.

Even though the Kinzies find they must keep expanding to meet the clamor for their unique candles, quality is still more important than quantiy and they intend to keep it that way. This year it is anticipated they will have to produce an average of 100 candles a day to meet their commitments, but each candle will be one-of-a-kind that will meet the high standards of Twi-Lite candles.

It is a well-known fact that the busiest people are always the ones who can find time for something else. The Kinzies give demonstrations for organizations, conduct candlemaking classes on a limited basis, and carry on correspondence with candlemakers throughout the çountry. Col. Kinzie is also Treasurer of the International Guild of Candle Artisans.

Although the Twi-Lite candle is now principally the candle with the antique glass pattern, Mrs. Kinzie still hand paints designs on other candles and creates original candles for special occasions.

The Kinzies have this to say about their business, "We really haven't had too many problems because what started as a hobby just mushroomed beyond anything we ever dreamed of or even really desired. However, we are a little smug about the fact that two old retirees past 60 started from scratch and in four years produced a business that is outgrowing them. Mostly we are pleased at creating something lovely that is completely our own idea."

Illustration No. 50. Some of the finished products of Twi-Lite Candles.

George and Irene Kinzie are living proof that hard work, attention to detail, and a fresh approach will create a demand for candles, or anything else, in an age when we are surrounded by all sorts of things bearing a rubber-stamp look. With their insistence upon individuality and originality and their willingness to devote the necessary time to produce unique, hand-crafted candles, the Kinzies and Twi-Lite Candles will be operating for a long, long time. (Illustration Nos. 48, 49, and 50).

The B & R Candle Shop

Two ladies from Syracuse, Kansas, combine their talents and abilities in what is probably unique in candle operations—The B & R Candle Shop. Rowena James and Betty Shetterly each have a candle business in their homes and these shops are separate and independent businesses. However, when the Christmas season approaches, they combine forces, move their candles to town, and are then known as the B & R Candle Shop. Each year they work with the Chamber of Commerce and local business firms to promote selling for Christmas. As an example of how this type of work and publicity pays off, last year during a dollar-day promotion they set up shop in the lobby of the Ames Hotel and had to go out of business before the day was over. Each had taken around 300 candles and they sold out before it was time to close up shop.

About fifteen years ago a friend gave Mrs. James a piece of wax and an instruction book, and that was the beginning of a very successful part-time career in candles. Her first display was in the window of her husband's newspaper office. Betty Shetterly saw her display and was inspired to begin her candlemaking efforts.

Even fifteen years ago Betty and Rowena were busy women. Both of them knit and sew; Rowena plays the organ, keeps house, and works with ceramics as well as candles; Betty works part time in a local hospital, does textile painting, and is active in club work. About five years ago they finally found the time to work together on candles and their lives have not been quite the same since.

They opened their shop in a room that was no longer needed by the James' son and an ad was placed in the Syracuse Journal. They sat and waited for the customers but none came. After

Illustration No. 51. Betty Shetterly with some of her lovely candles.

Illustration No. 52. The prize-winning candles of Betty Shetterly.

waiting a few weeks, they decided more drastic action was necessary so they had an open house, served coffee and cookies, and gave door prizes.

This launched the B & R Candle Shop so successfully that they had to work day and night to keep up with the demand for their candles. Since then they have tried to anticipate how many candles they will sell during the rush holiday season, but it seems that using last year's sales as a guideline doen't work, as they never make quite enough candles. One of these days they will probably have to abandon their individual businesses and combine forces in January to be properly prepared for the following December.

At the second annual convention of the International Guild of Candle Artisans held in Decatur, Alabama, Betty was named Candlecrafter of the Year. This was no small honor as the competition was keen and extremely professional. She entered candles in two categories and won blue ribbons on each, becoming the only double winner at the convention. Her grand prize winner was a white, thirteen-inch-high oval with hand carved sunflower and wheat, emblematic of the State of Kansas, with the designs painted in gold, yellow, brown, and green. This candle was presented to Alabama Governor Wallace and later a duplicate was presented to the Governor of Kansas. Her blue ribbon winner in the "most original" category was an 8-inch beeswax world globe with the continents overlaid in gold.

The children of both of these women are now married and no longer live at home, but at the beginning of their candlemaking careers they had to cope with all the problems of raising a family, running a household, keeping up their social contacts, and still they found time to build up a joint and a separate business that now consume a great deal of their lives.

The B & R Candle Shop and Twi-Lite Candles are just two of many examples of what can be done to make money with candles. The profiles of George and Irene Kinzie, and Betty Shetterly and Rowena James are included in this book to inspire the reader who is doubtful of his abilities and to prove that success in candlemaking is limited only by willingness to learn, experiment, and improve. (Illustration Nos. 51, 52, and 53.)

Illustration No. 53. Rowena James presenting some of her wax-decorated candles.

APPENDIX

International Guild of Candle Artisans

THE International Guild of Candle Artisans was formed in 1965 by a group of candlecrafters interested in the advancement and improvement of the art of creating candles. The principal objective of the Guild is the establishing and maintaining of high standards of candlecrafting among its members.

The Guild is composed of skilled professionals, hobbyists, and struggling beginners. The members are dedicated candlemakers who have banded together to share their knowledge and experience and to provide a clearing house for an exchange of ideas. Anyone who is interested in candlemaking is eligible for membership in the Guild.

Each year a convention is held in a different city in the United States with workshops, displays of new supplies, demonstrations of techniques, and talks on all that is new or interesting in the candlemaking world. There are also regional meetings for those who are unable to attend the annual convention.

Any member interested may join one of the Round Robins that circulate constantly. Each Robin is composed of six people and as each member of the group receives the Robin, he or she adds a letter illustrating a new candle, telling about a different idea, enclosing an interesting newspaper clipping relating to candles, giving information about a new material, or anything else that might be of interest to others in the group. The Robin completes its rounds with each member removing his old copy as it returns to him, adding something new and sending it on its way again.

Membership also includes receiving the Candleliter, which is the official publication of IGCA. The Candleliter presents news on activities of various members, interesting candlecrafting articles, and excerpts from all the Robins so that every member receives the benefit of the exchange of ideas in each Robin. The Candleliter also has a question and answer section. Any IGCA member who has a problem or a question may have it inserted in the Candleliter for a quick solution or answer.

For members who wish to sell their candles, the Guild will make every effort to locate sales outlets for them. Another function of the Guild it to locate and pass on to the members sources of supplies and equipment.

Eventually the Guild hopes to have an awards system so the members who work and develop their candlemaking ability can receive a certificate as they progress. This is in the future but is something that is being seriously discussed. The highest award of Master Candlecrafter will be a goal to strive for and will be worth all the learning, improving, and work it will require.

The Guild does not have a permanent mailing address, but any reader interested in joining IGCA or obtaining more information about it may write to me, Ruth Monroe, P. O. Box 3205, El Paso, Texas 79923.

List of Suppliers

Below is a list of suppliers who can furnish almost anything you might need for making and decorating candles. Some of these concerns have catalogs showing what they have available. There is a small charge for most of the catalogs and I suggest that you write and find out whether there is a charge before requesting catalogs.

Ceramic Molds

Duncan Ceramic Products, Inc.
5673 E. Shields Ave.
Fresno, California 93727

Candlemaking and Decorating Supplies

Pourette Manufacturing Co.
6818 Roosevelt Way
Seattle, Washington

Candlelite House
4228 E. Easter Place
Littleton, Colorado 80120

Wicks & Wax Candle Shop
350 N. Atlantic Avenue
Cocoa Beach, Florida 32931

Jo-Lann Ceramics & Gifts
569 A Grant St., S.E.
Atlanta, Georgia 30312

Lumi-Craft (Canada) Ltd.
P. O. Box 666
Kingston, Ontario, Canada

Cake Decorators & Craft Supplies
Blacklick, Ohio 43004

General Supplies Co.
P. O. Box 338
Fallbrook, California

Gold Foil Decorations

Harrower House of Découpage
River Road, Upper Black Eddy
Bucks County, Pennsylvania 18972

General Decorating Supplies

Lee Wards
840 North State St. (Rt. 31)
Elgin, Illinois 60121

Sea Life

Florida Supply House
P. O. Box 847
Bradenton, Florida

List of Foreign Suppliers

Handicraft Supply Pty.
35 Brighton Ave.
Croydon Park, N.S.W.
Australia

Myart Co. Pty. Ltd.
Box 3966 G.P.O.
Sydney, New South Wales
Australia

S. A. Jackson & Co. Ltd.
P.O. Box 3633
Auckland, C.I. New Zealand

Camp-O-Matic Ltd.
P.O. Box 21
Lansdowne
Capetown, South Africa

INDEX